Grilling with Beer

Bastes, BBQ Sauces, Mops, Marinades & More Made with Craft Beer

BY LUCY SAUNDERS

Publication Date: 2006

Publisher: F&B Communications

ISBN 10: 0-9769875-0-3

ISBN 13: 978-0-9769875-0-5

Suggested categories: Grilling, Outdoor Cookery, Craft Beer

Library of Congress Control Number: 2006907409

224 pages, more than 110 recipes, index

Website: www.grillingwithbeer.com

Email: grillingwithbeer@yahoo.com

Printed in Canada

Dedication

For my father, Bill Saunders, who taught me how to grill (and much more), with love

Cover Photography: Jennifer Marx

Design and Illustration: Libby VanderPloeg

Editing: Pamela McManus, Sandra Wu

Food Photography: Enji, enji.com

Food Stylist: Claire Stancer

Prop Stylist: Megan Szasz

Props: Upstairs at Pierre Lafond of Santa Barbara, California

Printing: The Hignell Book Company, Winnepeg, Manitoba, Canada

Website hosting: Intracommunities.org and Yahoo! Stores

ACKNOWLEDGMENTS

Thanks to the Alström Brothers and Michael Jackson for the prefaces. Thanks to contributors Anne and Brian Ausderau, Jay Brooks, Stan Hieronymus, Jack Kenny and Dan and Karen Rabin. Both photographers, Jen Marx and Angela Park, put in extra time and effort, with wonderful results. Thanks to Rainbow Graphics and Iridio for the color advance proofs. Bryan Rice deserves thanks for extensive research and print production. I am grateful to Angie Bell, Deb Carey, Tom Dalldorf, Charles Finkel, Rex Halfpenny, Tim Harper, David Hayes, Paul Joannides, Ashton Lewis, John Mallett, Lisa Morrison, Luke Nicholas, Eric Nielsen, Bill Owens, Daphne Scholz, and Steven White, for comments, fact-checking and reviews.

Many thanks to artist Libby VanderPloeg, who spent vast amounts of time researching fonts, turning page proofs, and creating wonderful illustrations and spot art in addition to her talented designs.

Generous recipe contributors include: Jay Brooks, brookston.org; Lew Bryson, lewbryson.com; Fred Bueltmann, New Holland Brewing Co.; Kevin Cousins, South Shore Brewery; Lee Custer, walksinshadows.com; Eric Gillish, Union Café and Millenium Restaurant Group; Lisa Aspenson, Mona Lisa Bistro; Cheryl and Bill Jamison, Smoke & Spice; Marc Kadish, Sunset Grill; Jenn Kolthoff and Mario Gongora, Marin Brewing; Daniel Leff; Gene Mueller, Flying Fish Brewery; Brian Morin, beerbistro; Gary Marx, Pike Pub; Randy Mosher, radicalbrewing.com; Scott McGlinchey, Q; Eric Nielsen, Shelton Bros. Imports; Owen Ogletree, classiccitybrew.com; Ric Orlando, New World Home Cooking; Bruce Paton, www.beer-chef.com; Jill Ramiel, Silver Bow Inn; Steven Raichlen, barbecuebible.com; and Terri Wuerthner.

Recipe testers include Marietta Abrams, Peter and John Brill, Angie and Larry Bell, Kerry Byrne, Lee Custer, Steve Gamble, Shawn Jeffries, Angela Johnson-MacArthur, Marc Kadish, Adrienne Lee, Anne Maedke, Julie McDonald, Lee Mathis, Chef Bruce Paton, Dan Rabin, Emily Romain, and Gary and Sona Rejebian, and others – thank you!

Thanks to: Dave and Diane Alexander, Toni Allegra, Fal Allen, Steve Barasch, Lori Barthelemy, Steve Beaumont, Angie & Larry Bell, Bev Bennett, Sally Bernstein, Dan & Julie Bradford, Bill Brand, Dennis Buettner, Sebbie Buhler, Kerry Byrne, Michael Chu, Sid Cook, Bill Daley, Ray Daniels, Sheana Davis, John DeMers, Gordon Edgar, Anne Elias, Gaylon Emerzian, Teri Fahrendorf, Toni Fladmark, Paul Gatza, Dan George, Chuck Hahn, Mike Hennick, Sara Hill, Cheryl Jamison, Jim Javenkoski, Gail Jennings, Jaime Jurado, Greg Kitsock, Michael Kuderka, Andrew Larsen, Peggy Leinenkugel, Dave Leonhardi, Lara Mackey, Tony Magee, Garrett Marero, Liz Melby, Bill Metzger, Alec Moss, David Mustard, Eric Nielsen, Barb Ostmann, Larry Perdido, Tom Peters, Nancy Piho, Erin Rutherford, Fred Scheer, Daphne & Richard Scholz, Carol Selva Rajah, Elise & Marty Roegnik, Pete Slosberg, Paris & Richard Steuven, Nancy Stohs, Brett Stubbs, Ron Tanner, Bill Taylor, Kate Theis, Wendy Tucciarone, Angela Wagner, Carol Wiley Lorente, Tom Willett, Mike Zeller, the Weber-Stephens Company for funding the fellowship for food writing on outdoor cookery, Sandy Wright and the Communications Arts/Writer's Colony at Dairy Hollow.

With love and gratitude to family and friends, especially Tom for all his patience, proofreading, help with printing and taste-testing, and much more, Bill & Sally, Margery, Kris & Maia, Tony & Amy, Julia, Katerina, Brit & Annabelle, Ginna and Bob, Gretchen, Wes, Lisa, & Piper, Mark & Kate, Sarah, Jeff & Ryan, Sona & Gary, Roger & Gaylon, Elise, Hal, and the Budd, Carter, Miller, Piper, Saunders, Theis, and Woodruff families.

Recipes & Reviews

Craft Beer:

the best thing to happen to the grill

The combination of drinking beer and grilling meat is one of those quintessential, recreational past-times. There's something ancestral about it. We're sure many of you have summertime memories of sucking back ice-cold fizzy, yellow, cheap beer while charring burgers, hot dogs and chicken on the hibachi.

Thankfully, times change.

Grills, cooking techniques, food options and eating habits have all evolved, and so has beer. Forget the typical beers you see mass-marketed on TV or in magazines. North America is now home to nearly 1,500 craft breweries that are brewing hundreds of different beer styles under thousands of different brands of flavorful craft beer — not to mention the thousands of craft beers imported from abroad. This reawakening of our beer palate has made craft beer one of the most complex and versatile beverages on the planet, and the perfect, and natural, choice when pairing or cooking with food!

What's craft beer?

Some try to define it by how many barrels of beer a brewery produces per year, but that doesn't cut it for us. Craft beer stems from a concept of brewing, or rather a brewing attitude, where taste, quality, creativity and passion reign and its masters are true artisans. Craft brews are generally handcrafted, in single batches, properly served, and rely on taste versus marketing. And despite what many think, craft beer is not a new trend or an isolated American fad. The concept of craft beer has been around for thousands of years.

The flavors and aromas found in craft beer range from fruity, floral, citrusy, sweet, sour, spicy, herbal, earthy, toasty, roasted, smoky, burnt, with textures from syrupy and rich to effervescent and delicate, thanks to the infinite combinations of malted and unmalted grains, hops, spices and other flavorings, water sources, yeast, bacteria and creative brewing techniques. You simply won't find this diversity with any other beverage.

Given this, beer should be considered a main ingredient, the "sauce of life," as it complements and enhances your enjoyment of food, and life. Especially when grilling. Trust us. The possibilities are literally endless. Whether you're making beer-based sauces, marinades, brines or

condiments, searing fish, tenderizing beef, broiling veggies, caramelizing, bathing brats, swabbing chops, misting ribs, or seasoning poultry, beer always has a place at the grill and will no doubt bring a unique depth to your food and grilling experience.

Lucy Saunders has been changing the way we think about and use craft beer for some 20 years — as a cook, columnist and teacher. We got hooked on her first book, Cooking with Beer, back in 1996, when Lucy opened our eyes to using beer in the kitchen by providing us with essential basics, solid recipes and plenty of tips. In Grilling with Beer, Lucy has captured the passion and fun found within both the art of grilling and craft beer. Her breadth of recipes, love for food and beer, and presentation of it all, leaves you hungry and rushing to the grill with beer in hand. And that's exactly what we did when we received her new recipes!

Coffee Stout Q Sauce (page 42) immediately caught our eyes. We used a rich and strong American Double Stout and some freshly brewed espresso, which melds into one, providing a sweet, roasty and smoky character that plays off caramelized onions and hints of molasses, while bacon, Worcestershire sauce and hot pepper sauce fuse for a slightly salty, and spicy, heated edge. We lathered the completed sauce on some beef flank steak rolls and grilled them up. The sweet, roasted and smoked flavors became more intense and

complemented the charring and saltiness of the meat—as it was meant to be—and we paired it with the same leftover stout. A most awesome combination of flavors and definitely a BBQ sauce that we'll be making plenty more of!

We also thoroughly enjoyed Lucy's recipe for Herbed Ale Brats (page 194) by cooking them in one of our favorite American Pale Ales. The beery flavors soak into the brats, keeping them extremely juicy on the grill, while the herb sauce of relish, garlic, parsley, marjoram, salt and pepper complements and draws out the hoppy, spicy and subtle sweet, malty notes of the beer. A very delicious and easy recipe that livens-up typical brats and will no doubt be a massive hit at any cookout!

If you're reading this and deciding whether or not to purchase this book, proceed to the checkout counter now. This book is a must for any food, grill, or beer enthusiast.

Now go forth and grill with beer!

Respect Beer (and the Grill).

Jason and Todd Alström
Founders, BeerAdvocate.com

About the author, Lucy Saunders

By Michael Jackson

You want to know about Lucy? I loved Lucy the moment I encountered her in the food and drink pages of the *Chicago Tribune*. She was saying the nicest things, in print, about my book The World Guide to Beer, which had just been published in its 1988 updated edition. In the Midwest, the beer revolution was still in its early days, but Lucy's review demonstrated a perfect understanding of my book.

A good-looking woman who understood me and praised me: men are notably susceptible to such a combination. A woman with good taste and judgment on the subject of beer: a matter of vital importance. Yes, it was love.

I invited Lucy to lunch at the Berghoff, in those days one of the few places in The Loop to serve interesting beers and good food. We had halibut sandwiches and the house wheat beer.

In the early 1990s, Lucy came to London and attended a dinner at the White Horse, in Parson's Green. This pub, run by beer-loving foodie Mark Dorber, was already famous for menus combining his passions. That evening, he served grilled lamb chops marinated in Mackeson, the classic (if under-appreciated) sweet stout. The lamb was garnished with rosemary, and served with very buttery mashed potatoes. Lucy loved the dish, and found a new friend in Mark. She later worked as an intern in the kitchen at the White Horse. I subsequently introduced her to Brussels' best known home of cuisine á la bière, In't Spinnekopke, where she cooked and studied the recipes of owner Jean Rodriguez.

In 1996, her first book, Cooking with Beer, was published by Time-Life Books. That work is a good, solid, information-packed guide. Now Lucy focuses on one particular starring role for beer. Her early encounters with grilling developed into a passion and now a book in its own right. It is a timely work. Grilling is immensely popular and the choice of craft beers is enormous.

Cooking and eating should be fun. Lucy has done all the hard work for you: the study, the training, the experience. Now, let her take you by the hand, and you will become the casual supercook. Read Lucy's recipes for barbecues, picnics, family dinners and backyard gatherings and go start grilling. You, too, will love Lucy's perfect understanding of craft beer and the flavors of grilled food.

Michael Jackson is the world's leading writer on beer. His books include The Great Beer Guide and Whisky: the Definitive World Guide (both DK Inc, New York). The latter won the 2006 James Beard Award as the year's best book on drink.

Introduction

by Lucy Saunders

Why grill with beer?

The first time I spotted an ad for a fancy 6-burner grill with a bottle of wine and two stemmed goblets perched on its shiny stainless steel hood, something clicked inside me like an electronic ignition. "Why *wine*?" I fumed. Craft beer delivers the best flavors to go with barbecue and grilled foods.

What makes a craft beer so tasty with grilled fare? Specialty roasted barley malts in a cascade of caramel colors enhance the flavors of barbecued food. Hops that range from floral to citrusy to deeply astringent help cut through the fat of ribs and burgers. And carbonation completes the sensation of refreshment, readying you for yet another bite.

About craft beer flavors

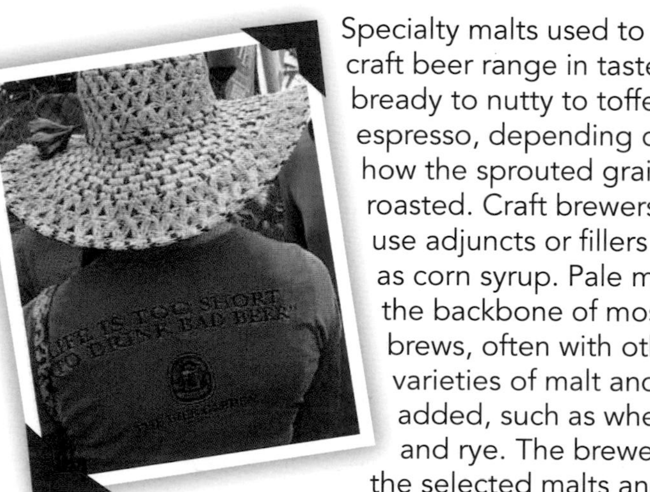

Specialty malts used to brew craft beer range in taste from bready to nutty to toffee to espresso, depending on how the sprouted grains are roasted. Craft brewers rarely use adjuncts or fillers such as corn syrup. Pale malt is the backbone of most craft brews, often with other varieties of malt and grains added, such as wheat, oats and rye. The brewer mills the selected malts and steeps the cracked kernels in hot water. An enzymatic

(continued on page16)

How to use this book

My goal is to introduce the flavors of craft beer into outdoor cooking, and encourage you to taste a variety of beer styles that is far more vast than you may realize. There are more than 100 recipes infused with the flavors of craft beer in this book, grouped in ten chapters. The first five chapters cover sauces, rubs, marinades and other recipes that can be used on many ingredients and in many ways. The final five chapters cover specific foodstuffs or preparations, such as chicken, seafood and burgers.

Some of the recipes are original; others are contributed and are noted as such. All have been taste-tested in home kitchens, thanks to more than two dozen fans of craft beer cuisine (see Credits).

Between chapters are profiles of popular festivals and events that feature craft beer and grilled or barbecued foods. Fests can highlight a specific style of beer, or the regional differences among craft brewers. They offer the fun of sampling many exotic styles of beer. Some, such as the Kona Brewers Festival, feature lots of different breweries from across North America. Others, such as the Harpoon Championships of New England Barbecue, feature lots of barbecue teams from around the region. And still others, such as the Park Hyatt's Blues, Brews, and BBQ festival at Beaver Creek, Colorado, feature regional breweries and chefs from around the country. Thanks to contributors Anne Ausderau, Jay Brooks and Dan Rabin for their fest reviews.

I have included a few reviews of international travels in search of both barbecue and craft beer, such as the Brightstone Brews, Blues & BBQs festival at Blake Park, Mt. Maunganui, New Zealand, and the James St. Cooking School class about craft beer and barbecue in Brisbane, Australia.

Appendices offer resources and pairing suggestions. Be sure to check out the safety tips on pages 20-22 and page 28, and visit grillingwithbeer.com for more information and recipes. —L.S.

reaction takes the malt starches and converts them into fermentable sugars. This process yields a sweet malty liquid called wort (pronounced "wert").

Wort can be a versatile ingredient for more than brewing beer. At a tasting of the Malt Shovel Brewery's craft beer, the chef prepared a barley wort sorbet with diced, ripe white peaches. It was a delicious counterpoint to spicy barbecue! And a concentrated form of wort, called barley malt extract, is a not-too-sweet substitute for molasses in sauces.

Malts in craft brews offer both robust taste and gravity. The gravity of a beer refers to the amount of sugar available for fermentation, and offers a clue to its final strength. A high-gravity beer offers both richer mouthfeel—thanks to dense sugars—and often higher alcohol content. Mass-market beer made with corn syrup or other simple sugars often taste thin and lack depth of flavor.

Other flavors in craft beer come from hops that are added in stages for bittering, spicy and aromatic effects that heighten the impact of seasonings in sauces and rubs. Most bottled beers are pasteurized, but some are bottle-conditioned with live yeast. Secondary fermentation with live yeast in the bottle yields gentle carbonation to contrast with juicy BBQ. Even if the beer is filtered and pasteurized, yeast esters remain to offer another dimension of taste.

Craft beer flavors enhance the caramelized, spicy taste of barbecued and grilled foods better than any other beverage. If you think I'm waving a freak flag with a culinary campaign for grilling with beer, think again. The doyenne of French cuisine, Julia Child, recommended a malty continental pilsner as the beverage of choice to go with grilled burgers and picnic fare.

But here's the gristly bit of truth: beer is such a classic partner to grilled and barbecued foods that it is shrugged off as ordinary, ho-hum, and so obvious as to be dull. "Yes, beer goes with everything," wrote Bill Daley of the *Chicago Tribune* in an article about summer barbecue. Can you hear the sigh?

Perhaps that's due to beer's common image and people's perceptions. Many people find mass-market beer advertising to be inane or silly (at best) or offensive and stupid (at worst). Some people still believe all beer tastes like fizzy malt water without a lot of flavor.

You call *this* beer?

Sometimes, just the brewer's craft and skill will create new flavors from the traditional four ingredients of malt, hops, yeast and water. The Flying Fish Brewing Co.'s Grand Cru Winter Reserve is fermented at a higher temperature than standard, adding an undercurrent of fruitiness (although there is no fruit in the beer). Very lightly filtered, the Grand Cru exhibits a complex mouthfeel, strong malt flavors, a spicy hop presence and warmth from the higher gravity, followed by a clean, dry finish. It's an excellent example of an American interpretation of a classic Belgian strong golden ale style.

Craft brewers often are extravagantly creative with ingredients and techniques. Such brews can be highly potent (such as Drake's Barley Wine or Dogfish Head's Raison d'Etre), brewed with malts smoked over peat or hardwoods (such as New Glarus Smoked Rye Bock or Stone Brewing Co.'s Smoked Porter), or aged for months in old brandy, whiskey or wine barrels (such as Tyranena Brewing Co.'s Rocky's Revenge Brown Ale). Or, craft beer can be flavored with espresso (such as the Meantime Coffee Porter), chocolate (such as Rogue Chocolate Stout), spices, exotic grains, berries, nuts (such as the Coconut Porter from Maui Brewing Co.) and even passionfruit (such as the Lilikoi Wheat Ale from Kona Brewing Co.).

Craft beers challenge the consumer perception of what a beer should be.

For example, try a hoppy IPA aged in white oak barrels once used to make chardonnay. Golden Valley Brewery of McMinnville, Oregon, makes an IPA VS Brut that straddles the line between wine's aromatics and beer's ingredients. It is perfumed with floral esters from the yeast used in fermentation and aromatic with aged hops, plus juicy notes from the addition of 2 bottles of Argyle Chardonnay into the fermentation tank. In short, it's a perfect contrast to the smoky flavors of grilled foods.

These are just a few examples from America's nearly 1,400 craft breweries, without considering the classic imported styles from other countries!

If your image of beer and barbecue is that of someone splashing a few suds on the grill from the same can used to swig back the drink, it's time to focus on flavor, first.

Outdoor cookery and craft beer

To give craft beer its due with barbecue, I thought, "Why not use it as an ingredient?" That way, people will sample the taste with other spices and seasonings. The surprise of sampling beer in barbecue could well awaken consumers to other craft beer pairings. So, I began grilling with beer in barbecue sauces, mops, marinades and more.

Turns out it's not such a novelty. In parts of Mexico and South America, marinating foods such as skirt steak, chicken, and seafood in dark lager is traditional preparation for the barbecoa or slow smoking over a wood fire.

I invited chefs and craft brewers alike to contribute their favorite recipes. Contributors are identified with bylines and, if available, links to their websites. One of the champions of better beer with wonderful cuisine is Brian Morin, of Toronto's beerbistro (yes, it's meant to be spelled with a lower case "b"). Chef Morin also contributes to the Mondial de la Bière Festival in Montréal, Quebec, which often features grilled foods.

The following chapters feature recipes that include the taste of different styles of beer. However, because of regional distribution and the fact that most craft brewers encourage you to "drink local," I don't make brand recommendations for pairings. Instead, I suggest you sample the final dish with the beer used to prepare it, as well as a contrasting

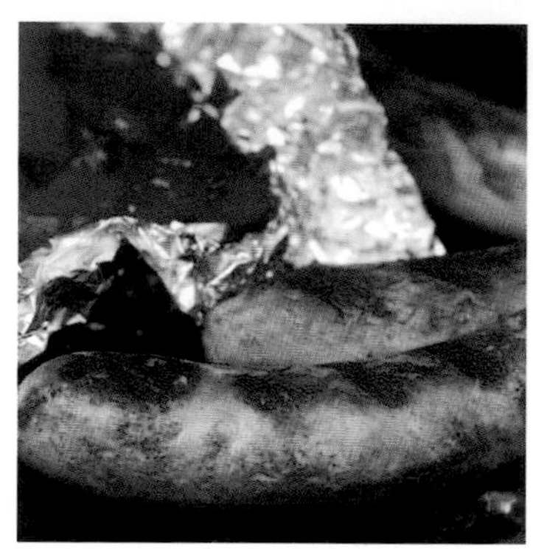

or complementary style. After sampling small tastes, you can choose which style of brew you prefer—the complement or the contrasting flavor.

Because all people taste things differently, try several styles of beer when creating your own food and beer pairings. For less than the cost of a good bottle of wine, you can buy several different brews to sample and share. Refer to the chart in Appendix I for pairing suggestions, offered by beer journalist, Stan Hieronymus, of appellationbeer.com. Or turn to the Brewers' Association, for a guide by tasting expert Randy Mosher, with pairings for dozens of dishes, sold online at www.beertown.org.

How to grill

Yes, grilling is dangerous—it involves sharp objects, raw meat, flames, fuel, and the realization that, with mere moments of inattention, your tasty steak can turn into nasty cinders.

My goal is to introduce the flavors of craft beer into barbecue. So, the recipes that follow assume a basic knowledge of outdoor cookery. If you're new to grilling, a pictorial guide by Steven Raichlen, How to Grill: The Complete Illustrated Book of Barbecue Techniques (Workman Publishing, 2001, $19.95), offers a fantastic introduction. You can also check out his website, www.bbqu.net, for cooking demonstrations and tips.

Here are more hints, adapted from the Hearth, Patio, & Barbecue Association's recommendations:

- First, understand now how your grill works (i.e., read the manual or ask someone knowledgeable for a demonstration). Place grill on level surface, away from wood siding, branches, walkways, paths or areas where children and pets play, and clear of swinging doors and windows. Cook outdoors, because carbon monoxide can kill you. And never leave a grill unattended once it's been lit, and especially after you've started cooking.

- Have a bucket of sand and fire extinguisher within easy reach. Have heavy-duty foil and long-handled tongs to move foods away from flare-ups. Foil drip trays help collect fat and prevent it from igniting.

- Dress the part. Roll up sleeves, pull back hair, and wear shoes. Use safe utensils that are sturdy and long-handled to keep out of reach of the heat. Avoid plastic or wood that might melt or scorch. Use nonflammable hot pads and mitts to protect hands.

- Keep grill grate clean to prevent cross-contamination of foods. If cooking for a crowd, use foil or grill trays to prevent raw or partially cooked meats or poultry from dripping on almost cooked foods. Use large pans and trays to transport cooked foods, with rims wide enough to carry without burning your hands.

- What is the best fuel for grilling? It depends on your tastes, time, gear and location. I use portable gas at the cabin in the woods (to prevent sparks) and when traveling. I use natural wood when there's time to tend the fire and it's safe to do so (no drought and therefore no risk of fire from wafting sparks). And I use charcoal when I want my food to have some smoky flavor but need the speed and convenience of the lump product. I don't use chemical-soaked briquettes, but do rely on a charcoal chimney that uses crumpled newsprint to start fires.

- Allow coals to burn out completely and let the ashes cool before disposing of them. I put ashes in a metal pail and cover them with dirt, soak the mixture and put it on the compost heap. Or, bury ashes in sand to smother any sparks. Do not put ashes or coals in a bucket of water, because stray sparks and residual heat creating steam may scald you.
- Before cooking on a gas grill, read the manual and know how to operate both the tank or fuel supply and the unit. Check all the connections and hoses before lighting. Keep the lid open when lighting it, and then cover to heat to desired temperature. Don't lean over the grill when lighting it. And if the burner won't light right away, turn off the gas, wait 5 minutes, and try again.
- Save the pint you drink for after you've finished cooking, particularly if grilling at high temperatures. Slow reflexes will lead to overcooked or burned food. (If you're barbecuing a haunch of beast for hours over a pile of smoking hardwoods, then that's another story....)
- Get a food thermometer and use it to check that internal temperatures of meat and poultry have reached a food-safe temperature before serving. The USDA has a chart of safe temperatures: http://www.fsis.usda.gov/Fact_Sheets/Barbecue_Food_Safety.

Grills come in all shapes and sizes, and often have prices to match. As someone on a beer budget, I ooh and aaaah over the big, fancy grills, but don't actually own one. I have a simple trolley-style barbecue that lets me smoke, grill and barbecue "low and slow," plus a 30-year old kettle grill. When I travel, I cook on a gas grill. Gas grills are convenient, often portable, and a few models are even affordable. A friend of mine went shopping for grills recently, and here's his story.

Bringing home the Q

"We had been shopping around last year for a new grill to replace the old monster. Our first visit was to a new shop in Westport, Connecticut dedicated to grills only. The first price tag we spotted read $3,200. Uh-oh. When we told the salesman our price range, he steered us to the "entry level models". Entry level!

After visits to a few more places, with similar experiences, I went to my local hardware store, a tiny place, and the one guy in Norwalk who hasn't been put out of business by Home Depot. He pulled a Weber Q off the shelf and asked if I knew about it. I was smitten immediately, and bought it.

There are several cool things about it. You can hook up your standard propane tank to it, or you can use a small propane canister, like those used for blow torches. The drippings pan removes easily, and uses a standard foil rectangular pan insert. The grill plate itself is heavy iron, not bulky, but requires some strength to lift.

I bought the rolling stand that Weber designed for it, which is not ideal but will do. They tell you not to put your propane tank on the shelf down by the wheels, but it fits there and so it now lives there. And I bought a cover for the grill as well (got a great bargain online).

Weber makes a few models of the Q. Mine is the standard one. Total cost about $230: $180 plus $50 for the two accessories. When you think about it, you can get a large rolling grill for that amount of money, but you can't carry it into the house and store it neatly away. And it's cute, sorta looks like a little visitor from space.

And the big question is How well does it perform?

Answer: Excellent. Nice, even distribution of heat. It's a fairly conservative flame, not at all scary. Let it heat up for 10-15 minutes and your grilling will go relatively fast.

by Jack Kenny, Beer Writer

Grilling at The Writers' Colony at Dairy Hollow

The book you now hold began to take shape at the Writers' Colony at Dairy Hollow in Eureka Springs, Arkansas. In early 2005, I won the Weber Fellowship for Food Writing on Outdoor Cookery, and spent a month in the *Renovation Style* Culinary Suite, developing new recipes, grilling, taste-testing, and writing.

The fellowship gave me a much-needed respite, peace and privacy, and the chance to explore the beauty of Arkansas in between batches of barbecue sauce. I made good friends there, and came away filled with gratitude for the space to cook in the gorgeous kitchen and work in the writing studio.

That's just why the place is there, in the words of one of the founders:

"Above all, I am a writer and illustrator and person of creative abilities and bent. I value that process and know it deserves to be nurtured and protected. It is that endorsement and refuge which we are ultimately working to provide here at our Writer's Colony."

—*Ned Shank, August, 2000*

The roots of the Colony unite the worlds of creativity and culinary arts. Built from a successful bed-and-breakfast run by Ned Shank and his wife, cookbook author and poet Crescent Dragonwagon, it seems natural that the Culinary Suite is part of the Writers' Colony.

Thanks to *Renovation Style* magazine, the efforts of then-editor Ann Maine, KitchenAid, Weber-Stephen, and kitchen designer Deborah Krasner, the Culinary Suite is a beautiful setting for writing about all things edible. The founders, board and staff of the Communication Arts Institute operate the Writers' Colony at Dairy Hollow and its programs. Set in the Ozark Mountains, the Colony offers one- to three-month residencies for working writers, artists and composers.

Since opening in 2000, the Colony has hosted more than 175 writers from around the world. The deck with the sparkling new Weber Summit grill is a wonderful place to gather, cook, talk, eat and write.

For more information about the Writers' Colony at Dairy Hollow, visit www.writerscolony.org.

BBQ Sauces

Thousands of brands of barbecue sauces crowd shelves at supermarkets around the globe, so why bother to make your own? Because the fresh flavor of real beer is superior in a homemade sauce! Plus, you can adjust the intensity of ingredients and seasonings to make it as spicy as you like.

Even big brewers acknowledge the allure of brewed BBQ: at press time, Anheuser-Busch launched a line of Bud-based BBQ sauces. The international brewery joins the company of many craft brewers, such as Gritty McDuff's of Freeport, Maine, and Sprecher Brewery of Glendale, Wisconsin, that have offered bottled or house-made "beer-b-cue" sauces for years.

Barbecue sauces tend to be thick, rich in flavor, and best suited to adding in the last 5 to 10 minutes of cooking, depending on the heat. That gives the sauce time to caramelize on the surface of the grilled foodstuff, without turning black and cindery. If your barbecue sauce is very sugary, apply over indirect heat to prevent flare-ups. Make extra sauce to pass at the table.

If faced with the last spoonfuls of a bottle of store-bought barbecue sauce, you might try thinning it with just a bit of beer to make it more spreadable. The beer adds aroma and flavor, and helps the bottled sauce flow evenly over the grilled foods.

Porter Plum Barbecue Sauce

Some taste-testers didn't like the flecks of plum skin in the sauce, and suggested peeling the plums for smoother texture. I didn't bother, because I like the intense flavor of the sun-ripened skin. But it's your choice, so if you want a velvety smooth sauce, just purée well and push the purée through a fine mesh sieve. Brush on pork tenderloin, chops, smoked shoulder or beef ribs during last 10 minutes of cooking.

- 1 tablespoon toasted sesame oil
- 2 tablespoons minced onion
- 2 very ripe black plums, pitted and chopped (8 ounces)
- 8 ounces porter
- 1 tablespoon black bean garlic sauce
- 1 teaspoon grated fresh tangerine or orange peel
- ½ teaspoon ground red cayenne pepper
- 1 tablespoon honey
- Salt and pepper to taste

1. Place oil, onion and plums in medium saucepan and cook over low heat until onions are soft.

2. Add porter, black bean garlic sauce, tangerine and cayenne. Simmer until plums are soft, about 5 minutes, but do not let boil. Place in blender and purée on HIGH until liquefied.

3. Return to saucepan and add honey, salt and pepper to taste. Simmer until thickened.

Makes 1½ cups.

> Safety tip: Cover blender lid with a folded tea towel and hold lid in place when mixing warm liquids. The heat generates steam that may expand and push off the blender lid. Hold lid in place firmly during operation.

Porter Plum Barbecue Sauce

Smoked Ale Mustard Sauce

Although imported German rauchbiers can be difficult to find, there are wonderful dark ales made with smoked malts brewed in North America. Sip just a bit of the smoked ale before making this sauce to see how the flavor intensifies.

- ½ cup dark brown sugar
- 2 tablespoons unsweetened cocoa powder
- 12 ounces smoked ale or rauchbier
- ¾ cup brown mustard seeds
- ¼ cup melted unsalted butter
- 1 teaspoon salt
- ½ teaspoon hot pepper sauce
- 1 tablespoon minced shallot

1. Combine brown sugar and cocoa in a small bowl and press with back of spoon to remove any lumps. Stir rauchbier, brown sugar and cocoa powder together in a small saucepan over low heat. Whisk well. Simmer 20 minutes or until reduced by one-third, stirring occasionally.
2. In small skillet over medium heat, toast mustard seeds just until aromatic. Let cool and scrape the mustard seeds into blender. Add beer-cocoa mixture, butter, salt, hot pepper sauce and shallots to blender and blend on HIGH until smooth. Taste and adjust seasonings.

Makes 1½ cups.

Peppery Pilsner Barbecue Sauce

- ½ cup cider vinegar
- ½ cup sugar
- 1 tablespoon crushed red pepper flakes
- 2 tablespoons garlic, peeled and minced
- 1 cup minced yellow onion
- 1 cup tomato chili sauce or ketchup
- 8 ounces pilsner
- ⅓ cup Worcestershire sauce
- 1 tablespoon hot pepper sauce
- 2 tablespoons bourbon

1. Mix vinegar, sugar and pepper flakes in large saucepan over medium heat and cook 15 minutes. Add garlic, onions, tomato chili sauce, pilsner and Worcestershire sauce; simmer 20 minutes.
2. Add hot pepper sauce and bourbon; simmer 15 minutes more. Baste on grilled chicken or ribs during final 15 to 20 minutes of cooking over indirect heat. The sauce is sugary and will cause flare-ups if applied over direct fire.

Makes about 2½ cups.

Smoke & Spice Cinderella Sauce

The Jamisons are pioneers of outdoor cookery and gourmet cuisine. Cheryl Jamison is an inspiration to me: She is a female chef and teacher from whom I took a class 10 years ago. This recipe is from their award-winning book, Smoke & Spice. The introduction says: "We developed this originally for barbecued beef short ribs, but decided it was too good to limit to one dish. It also transforms other everyday cuts of meat, from pork spareribs to chicken drumsticks."

- 1½ cups ketchup
- 1 cup dark lager
- ¾ cup cider vinegar
- ¼ cup minced fresh cilantro
- 3 tablespoons packed brown sugar
- 2 tablespoon Worcestershire sauce
- 2 garlic cloves, minced
- 2 teaspoons ground cumin
- 1½ teaspoons ground anise seeds
- 1½ teaspoons salt
- 1 teaspoon hot pepper sauce

1. Mix the ingredients in a saucepan and bring the liquid to a simmer. Reduce the heat to low and cook the mixture until it thickens, approximately 40 minutes. Stir frequently. Use the sauce warm. It keeps, refrigerated, for a couple of weeks.

Makes about 2½ cups.

Pale Ale Ponzu Sauce

Not your typical ponzu sauce, the mixture of a floral pale ale and a splash of mirin is what makes it sweet. Try it with Elysian Jasmine IPA from Seattle, Washington, or a floral, dry hopped pale ale.

- ½ cup pale ale
- 2 tablespoons brown sugar or palm sugar
- ¼ cup fresh-squeezed grapefruit juice (⅓ to ½ grapefruit)
- 1 tablespoon fresh-squeezed orange juice (¼ orange)
- 2 tablespoons low sodium soy sauce
- 2 tablespoons mirin (sweet rice wine)
- 1 teaspoon cornstarch
- ½ teaspoon red pepper flakes
- ½ teaspoon black sesame seeds

1. Mix all ingredients in a small skillet and place over medium-low heat. Simmer and stir with a whisk until thickened, about 3 minutes.

2. Remove from heat. Taste and adjust seasonings. Use as a glaze for grilled salmon or swordfish during last 1 to 2 minutes of cooking. The glaze will have time to set, but if exposed to direct flame, the sugars will char.

Makes 1 scant cup.

Palm sugar is found in Asian food sections of large grocery stores, or by mail order. Its buttery rich flavor goes well with barbecue. Pale Ale Ponzu Sauce may also serve as a dipping sauce for spring rolls or grilled satay.

Peach Lambic BBQ Sauce

If you buy peaches by the basket, there are always some bruised and overripe fruit lurking near the bottom of the basket. Use blemished but otherwise tasty fruit to make this sauce.

- 3 cups peaches, peeled, pitted and chopped, with juices reserved
- 2 tablespoons malt vinegar
- 1 tablespoon butter
- 1 tablespoon canola oil
- 1 cup minced sweet onion, such as Vidalia
- 2 tablespoons minced shallots
- 1 teaspoon ground white pepper
- 1 teaspoon ground black pepper
- 1 teaspoon ground coriander
- ½ teaspoon ground turmeric
- ½ teaspoon ground allspice
- 1 teaspoon salt
- ⅓ cup tomato paste
- ⅔ cup spicy brown or grainy prepared mustard
- 12 ounces peach lambic or other fruity ale
- Several splashes Worcestershire sauce
- 1 tablespoon hot pepper sauce, or to taste

1. Toss chopped peaches and reserved juice with malt vinegar in large bowl and set aside.

2. In large, deep stockpot placed over medium-low heat, melt butter with canola oil, and add onion and shallots. Cook and stir 1 minute. Reduce heat to low, and add peppers, coriander, turmeric, allspice and salt. Stir well to coat onions and shallots, and simmer 2 to 3 minutes.

3. When onions are tender, stir in peaches with reserved juices, tomato paste, mustard, peach lambic, Worcestershire and hot pepper sauces. Simmer over low heat, uncovered, for 30 minutes, stirring occasionally. (Mixture can be cooked longer for a thicker sauce.) Use hand-held stick blender

to purée sauce to desired consistency. Taste and adjust seasonings. Makes an excellent baste for fish, poultry and pork.

Makes 4 cups.

Bourbon Bock BBQ Sauce

- ¼ cup minced garlic
- ½ cup minced peeled apple (Granny Smith works best)
- 2 minced jalapeño peppers (include seeds for hotter sauce)
- ¼ cup butter
- 12 ounces bock or dark lager
- 2 ounces bourbon
- 4 ounces tomato paste
- Black pepper and salt to taste

1. Place garlic, apple, jalapeños and butter in medium saucepan over low heat. Simmer, stirring often, until garlic is tender and just golden, about 6 minutes.

2. Add bock, bourbon and tomato paste. Cook over low heat until thickened and reduced by one-third. Let cool to lukewarm, and purée in blender on HIGH until smooth. Taste and add black pepper and salt to taste. Good on ribs, chicken and pork.

Makes 1¾ cups.

South Shore Stout BBQ Sauce

Kevin Cousins, sous chef at The Deepwater Grille & South Shore Brewery in Ashland, Wisconsin, shares his recipe for South Shore Stout BBQ Sauce, served on braised pork ribs at the restaurant. "It is a bold, semi-spicy sauce that would be great for many other meats and grilled foods," says Cousins. I tweaked the recipe by substituting cooked bacon for the liquid smoke and caramel sauce base used in the original. Or, add a splash of rauchbier with the stout for rich smoky flavors, and simmer a bit longer to reduce the sauce.

- 2 tablespoons melted butter
- 1 large yellow onion, peeled and minced
- 2 tablespoons minced garlic
- 2 tablespoons chili powder
- 1 tablespoon crushed red pepper flakes
- 1 teaspoon cayenne pepper
- 1 teaspoon ground coriander
- 1 teaspoon ground white pepper
- 2 teaspoons fresh ground black pepper
- 1 teaspoon celery salt
- 12 ounces stout
- ½ cup red wine vinegar
- ½ cup Worcestershire sauce
- 2 slices smoked bacon, cooked until brown, and crumbled
- ¼ cup honey
- ¼ cup molasses
- 2 bay leaves
- 28 ounces crushed tomatoes

1. In a large saucepan placed over medium heat, cook onions and garlic in butter until onions are translucent. Add all spices and cook and stir for 1 minute.

2. Increase heat to medium. Add all remaining ingredients.

Bring to a simmer and turn heat to very low. Simmer ½ hour, stirring often. Do not let bottom of saucepan burn or the sugars and tomatoes will caramelize.

3. Remove from heat and let cool to lukewarm. Strain through a fine mesh sieve.

Makes 4 cups sauce.

Classic City Sauce

Owen Ogletree is an evangelist for the cause of craft beer in Georgia, but he loves his BBQ, too. Here's a tangy sauce, originally made with Terrapin Wake-N-Bake Coffee Oatmeal Imperial Stout.

- ¼ teaspoon dried ground cumin
- ¼ teaspoon dried finely ground oregano
- ¼ teaspoon dried finely ground thyme
- ¼ teaspoon ground black pepper
- dash cayenne pepper
- ¼ cup apple cider vinegar
- ½ cup black strap molasses
- ⅛ cup Imperial Stout
- ¼ cup honey
- 1 cup prepared Dijon mustard
- 1 teaspoon butter

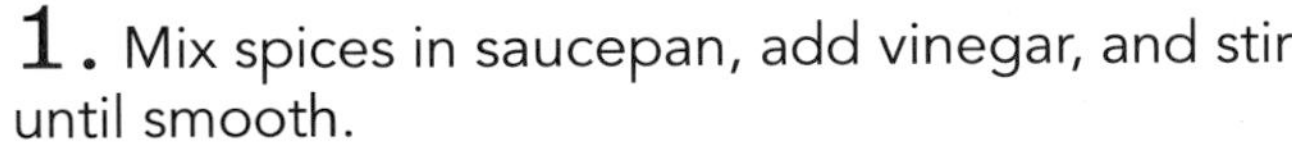

1. Mix spices in saucepan, add vinegar, and stir until smooth.

2. Add molasses, stout, honey and mustard; whisk well. Turn heat to low and bring to a simmer. Cook and stir 10 minutes and add butter. Simmer and stir about 5 more minutes.

Makes 2 cups.

Cherry Q Sauce

Sweet, sweet, sweet! Try this on grilled onions, chicken or even swordfish. If you like a strong fermented flavor, substitute a cherry kriek lambic for the amber ale.

- ⅓ cup cherry fruit-only spread
- 1 tablespoon dried cherries
- 2 tablespoons raspberry or cider vinegar
- 2 tablespoons butter
- 1 teaspoon salt
- 1 teaspoon ground white pepper
- ¼ teaspoon powdered mustard
- ¼ teaspoon dried thyme
- 1 teaspoon Worcestershire sauce
- 8 ounces amber ale

1. Place all ingredients in saucepan and simmer 15 minutes over low heat. Scrape mixture into blender and purée on HIGH until smooth.

Makes 1¼ cups.

Safety tip: Cover blender lid with a folded tea towel and hold lid in place when mixing warm liquids. The heat generates steam that may expand and push off the blender lid. Hold lid in place firmly during operation.

Cherry Q Sauce

Mexican Dark Lager Mole

- 2 tablespoons peanut oil
- 1 onion, chopped (6 ounces)
- 2 pasilla chiles, chopped and seeds reserved
- 2 cloves garlic, peeled and smashed
- 2 tablespoons paprika
- ¼ cup grated bittersweet chocolate
- 1 can (15 ounces) fire-roasted tomatoes with chiles
- 1 tablespoon ancho chile powder
- 2 teaspoons ground cumin
- 1 teaspoon dried oregano
- 1 teaspoon ground coriander
- Pinch cinnamon
- 12 ounces Mexican dark lager
- ⅓ cup sesame or pumpkin seeds
- 1 tablespoon canola oil
- Salt and black pepper to taste

1. Place peanut oil, onion and pasilla chiles in large deep skillet and cook and stir over medium heat 1 minute. Add garlic, paprika and chocolate. Cook and stir until onions are tender, about 3 more minutes. Place in blender and add tomatoes, chile powder, cumin, oregano, coriander and cinnamon. Cover and pulse on HIGH until mixed and chiles are finely chopped. Add lager to reach desired consistency, about 10 to 12 ounces. Return to saucepan.
2. In a small saucepan over low heat, toast sesame or pumpkin seeds with the reserved pasilla chile seeds; add just enough canola oil to keep seeds from sticking. When golden, stir seeds into simmering mole sauce. Taste and adjust seasonings. Simmer until thickened. Brush on grilled chicken or pork.

Makes about 2½ cups.

Sunset Grill Banana BBQ Sauce

If you have a few very ripe bananas on hand, skip the banana bread and make this BBQ sauce instead. This recipe is adapted from one shared by chef Marc Kadish, one of the champions of better beer in Boston, and owner of the fabled multi-tap, the Sunset Grill in Allston, Massachusetts.

- 6 ounces strong golden ale, such as dubbel
- 8 ounces ketchup
- 2 tablespoons brown sugar
- ¼ cup molasses
- 2 cups mashed ripe bananas
- ½ teaspoon ground black pepper
- ½ teaspoon salt
- 2 teaspoons minced garlic
- 2 tablespoons soy sauce
- 1 teaspoon ground ginger
- ¼ cup pineapple juice

1. Combine all ingredients in a large saucepan. Cook over low heat for 30 minutes, stirring often, until thickened and volume is reduced by one-quarter.

2. Let cool for 20 minutes. Purée in a blender on HIGH until smooth. Baste on grilled fish, chicken or pork.

Makes 3 cups.

Coffee Stout Q Sauce

An outstanding cooking and table sauce for BBQ pork or beef ribs, with bacon adding just the right hint of smoky flavor.

- 3 strips smoked bacon, chopped
- 2 cups chopped white onion
- 12 ounces stout
- ¼ cup espresso or very strong coffee, or 2 teaspoons instant espresso powder
- 2 tablespoons molasses
- 2 teaspoons Worcestershire sauce
- 2 tablespoons hot pepper sauce
- 1 teaspoon ground white pepper
- 1 teaspoon finely ground black pepper
- 1 cup ketchup
- 2 tablespoons malt vinegar

1. Place bacon in medium Dutch oven or heavy saucepan over medium-low heat. Cook and stir until bacon is golden and sizzling. Add onions; stir well to coat and cover. Reduce heat to low. Simmer until onions are caramelized, about 10 minutes.

2. Add remaining ingredients; stir well. Cook and stir 15 minutes and remove from heat. Use hand-held stick blender to purée in pot, or let cool and purée in batches in countertop blender.

3. Strain sauce to make smooth. Taste and adjust seasonings. Apply to ribs, pork or beef during last 10 minutes of cooking, over indirect heat. If sauce flares up, remove food to a sheet of foil placed over indirect heat on grill top. Do not let sauce burn.

> Note: To make a vegetarian version of this sauce, omit bacon and add smoked sea salt for smoky flavor.

Makes about 2½ cups.

Brian Morin's Barbeque Sauce

If you can't find apple ale, use a hard cider, or a mixture of 10 ounces amber ale and 2 ounces frozen apple juice concentrate.

- 2 tablespoons butter
- 2 cups yellow onion, peeled and diced
- ½ cup apple cider vinegar
- 3 cups apple ale
- Juice and zest of one half lemon, about 3 tablespoons juice
- 4 cups ketchup

1. Place all ingredients into large heavy pot, bring to a boil and reduce until sauce lightly coats the back of a wooden spoon. Strain through a fine strainer.

Makes 1 scant quart.

Kona Brewers Festival

Brings on the BBQ

True to its culinary roots, the biggest beer fest on the Big Island begins with a BBQ. The night before the Kona Brewers Festival, guests and brewers alike mingle with volunteers at a private dinner held behind the Kona Brewing Company. Guests dine on foods such as Smoked Big Wave Golden Ale Shoyu Chicken, Brewers Wort Potato Salad, and other treats. Arcs of lights strung along a wall of empty kegs transform the parking lot into a party, so brewers can relax before the big gig.

And it is a really big gig for good works: the Kona Brewers Festival has raised more than $225,000 for local charities, including a culinary scholarship program, in the 11 years of its existence. The 1-day event draws 1,800 fest goers to savor brews from all across Hawai'i, and North America, served alongside fabulous foodstuffs from ahi to truffles, donated by local restaurants.

"The Kona Brewers Festival offers terrific food, better beer, and more interesting chefs than any other," says Cameron Healy, one of the founders of the Kona Brewing Company, pictured here with Kona president, Mattson Davis.

Sited along the shore of a small jut of sand behind the King Kamehameha's Kona Beach Hotel, the festival is filled with booths offering grilled ribs, glazed shrimp, soft-shell crabs, even the traditional ahi tuna tartare known as "poke" served in savory waffle cones displayed in bowls of colorful Hawaiian salt.

Artfully carved melons and the Hawaiian salt display earned the Sheraton the "Aina Akamai" award for the most innovative tasting station at the 2006 fest. The serving cones were completely edible, taking top marks for earth-friendly presentation.

Since the local chapter of the American Culinary Federation always receives charitable donations from the festival's proceeds each year, all the food vendors are truly diverse. There was not a wedge of pizza to be had, not even any hot dogs.

Instead, dishes of different cuisines and spices were served with flair to fest goers, from pulled-pork barbecue served on palm fronds, to grilled shrimp over greens.

Ale-steamed sliced kielbasa was the most traditional beer fest foodstuff offered. All the choices appeared to fit the Hawaiian style of entertaining—whenever drinks are served, there are typically a few pupus, or bite-sized foodstuffs, offered to taste.

Imagine an appetizer menu filled with dozens of delights, and served along side sips of almost every kind of beer style. Taste a hugely hoppy Flying Fish IPA along with a spicy grilled focaccia—and then try a sip of Maui Brewing Co.'s award-winning CoConut Porter (a malted coco confection in a pint glass) with a chocolate truffle. The pairings seem endless, and the variety and fun makes it clear that this is no ordinary beer fest.

Another difference is the relative tranquility of the event. Most festivals start with a charge of fest-goers stampeding to the beer. But this fest starts with a ceremony that inspires and entertains. A traditional Hawaiian blessing, performed by local legend Kumu Hula Pekelo Day and a bevy of bare-shouldered dancers, winds up in a procession to the beach. Music, drums and chants invoke the island gods and goddesses to bring blessings to the party.

And instead of bins overflowing with refuse, numerous volunteers helped separate trash from recyclables to support Recycle Hawaii. The Trash Fashion Show was an hour's celebration of reclaimed and recycled materials turned into wearables (at least for the afternoon's entertainment).

Each year, a few new breweries join the camaraderie. Gene Mueller from the Flying Fish Brewing Co. of New Jersey flew the farthest to participate in the 2006 fest. He found the event "wonderful and exceeding all my expectations!"

Much of the delight is due to the rugged beauty of the Kona beach. With palm trees silhouetted on the skyline, warm breezes, boats and sunbathers strewn on the sand, it's truly a pint-lover's paradise. As the day winds on, drinkers begin to dance along to the tunes of slack key guitar and traditional Hawaiian music with encouragement from festival announcer and local DJ legend, Lyman Medeiros.

The spirit of the festival is friendly and fun. People delight in the craft beer and food served, and celebrate the aloha surrounding the event. Organizer Lara Mackey and a planning committee comprised of Kailua-Kona community members do much of the community outreach and coordination for the festival. Volunteers include the Kona Brewing Company's brewer Rich Tucciarone, and his wife Wendy, (pictured at right); though tired, they look happy and exultant at the end of the Fest!
—L.S.

WWW.KONABREWERSFESTIVAL.COM

Brew Bastes & Mops

Keep food moist on the grill with a baste or mop sauce made with craft beer, herbs and spices. Thin and liquid, a mop sauce adds flavor and moisture to foods cooked over low heat for a long time. Because it is typically less sugary than a standard barbecue sauce, a mop or baste can be applied repeatedly during grilling with less risk of flare-ups.

Both bastes and mop sauces are made to apply throughout the cooking time, not just at the end as with a traditional barbecue sauce. Because beer is about 90 percent water, it adds flavor with plenty of moisture to foods cooked slow in a traditional barbecue.

Because bastes and mop sauces are so thin and drizzly, they need the right tools to apply them to food surfaces to prevent them from dampening the fire. A mop utensil, made with a head of looped cotton string, helps swab on the baste or mop sauce without too many drips. A baste made with lots of herbs and seasonings can be applied with a silicone brush. Or, a very thin baste can be made with powdered herbs and beer, and splashed on with a condiment squeeze bottle fitted with a nozzle.

Apricot Ale Baste

If you can find an ale made with apricots, such as one made by Ithaca Brewing Co. or Pyramid Brewery, you may use it to enhance this fruity baste. If not, don't worry — this recipe uses dried apricots for real fruit flavor.

- 6 ounces dried apricots
- 12 ounces apricot ale or peach lambic
- 2 tablespoons toasted sesame oil
- 1 cup chopped onion
- ½ cup chicken stock
- 1 teaspoon yellow mustard seeds
- 1 teaspoon grated ginger
- 1 teaspoon pink peppercorns

1. Place apricots and apricot ale or peach lambic in 1-quart deep saucepan and simmer until fruit is soft. Add oil, onion and chicken stock. Simmer 5 minutes, then add all remaining ingredients. Cook, stirring occasionally, until apricot softens, about 5 minutes.
2. Scrape mixture into blender and purée on HIGH for 2 minutes, or until emulsified. May be used as a marinade for fish or as a basting sauce.

Makes about 2 cups.

You can find yellow mustard seeds and pink peppercorns at spice merchants online, or substitute a teaspoon of grainy seed mustard and ground black pepper. Pink peppercorns have a more subtle heat, so adjust seasoning as you taste.

Safety tip: Cover blender lid with a folded tea towel and hold lid in place when mixing warm liquids. The heat generates steam that may expand and push off the blender lid. Hold lid in place firmly during operation.

Apricot Ale Baste

Third Coast Seafood Baste

Chef Eric Gillish of the Union Café, Kalamazoo, Michigan, makes this citrusy emulsion with Bell's Third Coast Old Ale, a strong barley wine. Grate the zest off the citrus peel before squeezing out the juice.

- ½ orange, zested and juiced
- 1 small lemon, zested and juiced (Meyer lemon preferred)
- 1 small lime, zested and juiced
- 1 tablespoon fresh chopped thyme
- 2 tablespoons fresh chopped cilantro
- 1 tablespoon fresh chopped garlic
- 1 teaspoon ground cumin
- 1 tablespoon kosher or ground sea salt
- 1 tablespoon freshly ground black pepper
- 1½ cups olive oil
- 1 cup barley wine

1. Mix all ingredients in a blender until emulsified. Use as a baste for seafood such as shrimp or scallops. May also be used as a salad dressing.

Makes about 2 cups.

Fat Squirrel Satay Baste

Rich with nut brown ale and peanuts, this baste can be used on skewers of chicken tenders to make a satay-style appetizer. The name, Fat Squirrel, comes from the brand of brown ale made by the New Glarus Brewing Co. of Wisconsin.

- 2 teaspoons yellow Thai curry paste
- 1 teaspoon grated ginger
- 2 tablespoons fresh lime juice
- 2 tablespoons soy sauce
- ½ cup creamy peanut butter (natural ground is best)
- 2 tablespoons minced garlic
- 4 ounces coconut milk
- 4 ounces nut brown ale

1. Mix all ingredients in a saucepan over low heat. Cook and stir until peanut butter is melted. Remove from heat.
2. Let cool to lukewarm and purée in blender on HIGH until smooth. Use immediately.

Makes 1½ cups.

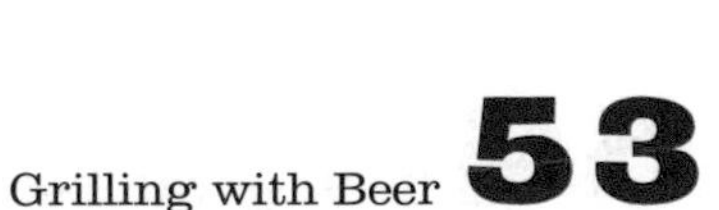

Thai Basil Ale Baste

If you love Thai curry, you'll like this piquant baste, fragrant with spicy Thai or holy basil. If you use broad-leaf basil, you'll find the flavor is not as intense.

- 3 cloves garlic, peeled and chopped
- 2 teaspoons grated ginger
- 2 tablespoons minced lemongrass (white portion of bulb)
- 1 teaspoon habañero pepper sauce, or to taste
- ½ teaspoon ground white pepper
- 2 teaspoons coconut oil
- ½ teaspoon salt
- 1 tablespoon palm sugar or cane syrup
- 1 cup unsweetened coconut milk
- 1 cup strong golden ale
- ¼ cup chopped Thai basil

1. Place garlic, ginger, lemongrass, habañero sauce and pepper in 1-quart saucepan. Add coconut oil and cook and stir over low heat until aromatic. Scrape into blender.

2. Add all remaining ingredients to blender and purée on HIGH until emulsified. Return to saucepan and cook over very low heat for 30 minutes; strain. Use to brush on fish or chicken.

Makes about 2 cups.

Thai ingredients can be hard to locate at your neighborhood market. If you can't find lemongrass, substitute 1 tablespoon lemon juice, and decrease the amount of ale by 1 tablespoon. Palm sugar adds both sweetness and fat, so if you can't find palm sugar, substitute 1 tablespoon sugar mixed with 1 teaspoon vegetable oil. True Thai basil really does make a difference to the taste of this baste, but Italian basil can be substituted - just add an extra tablespoon to punch up the flavor.

Lemon Lager Baste

An easy, herbal basting sauce for grilled vegetables.

1 tablespoon red pepper flakes
1 teaspoon ground black pepper
1 teaspoon salt
1 teaspoon celery seed
1 teaspoon coriander seed
1 tablespoon minced garlic
1 tablespoon grated lemon rind
2 tablespoons Italian flat-leaf parsley
4 ounces pilsner lager
4 ounces olive oil

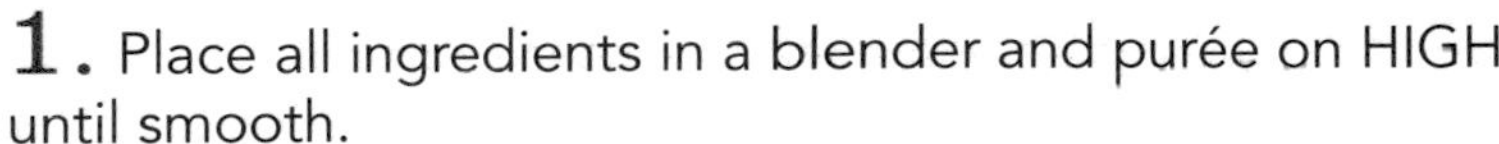

1. Place all ingredients in a blender and purée on HIGH until smooth.

Makes 1¼ cups.

Malted Mint Mop

Perfect for butterflied and grilled leg of lamb, or grilled game meats.

8 ounces stout or Belgian strong golden ale
2 tablespoons canola oil
1 teaspoon lemon juice
2 tablespoons minced green onion
2 tablespoons fresh mint leaves
1 teaspoon salt
1 teaspoon red pepper flakes (or to taste)

1. Place all ingredients in blender and purée on HIGH until smooth. Use immediately.

Makes 1 cup.

Jamison's Basic Beer Mop

Anything from barbecued Texas brisket to pork butt will happily lap up this brew, mopped on to smoked food while it cooks to add moisture and flavor. If you think more spice is nice, add a few slices of pickled or fresh jalapeño or serrano chile.

- 12 ounces pilsner
- ½ cup cider vinegar
- ½ cup water
- ¼ cup vegetable oil
- ½ medium onion, chopped or sliced in thin rings
- 2 garlic cloves, minced
- 1 tablespoon Worcestershire sauce
- 1 tablespoon dry rub or other dry seasoning blend that complements the flavor of your dish

1. Combine ingredients in saucepan. Heat mop and use warm, brushing onto food while smoking with a small string mop or basting brush.

Makes about 3 cups.

From Smoke & Spice, copyright 2003, Cheryl and Bill Jamison, published by Harvard Common Press.
Used with permission from author.

Golden Chipotle Mop

This mixture does double-duty as a salad dressing.

- 1 tablespoon powdered chipotle chiles
- ½ cup minced onion
- 1 tablespoon minced garlic
- ⅓ cup canola oil
- 2 tablespoons sun-dried tomatoes packed in oil
- 2 tablespoons malt vinegar
- 1 tablespoon sorghum or dark honey
- 4 ounces dark lager
- 1 tablespoon tomato paste

1. Place chipotle, onion, garlic, canola oil, and sun-dried tomatoes in a quart saucepan over low heat. Cook and stir until onions are tender, about 5 minutes. Remove from heat.

2. Add vinegar, sorghum or honey, lager and tomato paste; stir well. Let cool to lukewarm. Scrape mixture into blender and purée on HIGH until smooth. Use as a mop.

Makes 1 scant cup.

Brewer Ashton Lewis of the Springfield Brewing Company, Missouri, recommends that this mop sauce be used over indirect heat, because the sugars may caramelize quickly and flare up if applied over open flames.

Strong Cider BBQ Baste

Strong "syder" is the focus of a tasting competition in Michigan, a state famed for its apples. Rex Halfpenny, the editor of the Michigan Beer Guide, is a fan of strong cider in cooking, and this sauce adds plenty of apple nuances to a tangy sweet baste. Apply it over chicken, pork or even tempeh on the the grill, during the final 10 minutes of cooking.

- 2 tablespoons canola oil
- ½ cup chopped white onion
- 2 tablespoons minced garlic
- 1 tablespoon molasses
- 2 tablespoons hot or sweet paprika
- 1 tablespoon ground black pepper
- 1 teaspoon powdered hot mustard
- 1 tablespoon sugar
- 1 teaspoon salt
- 12 ounces strong cider
- 1 can (6 ounces) tomato paste
- Several dashes Worcestershire sauce, to taste

1. Place canola oil in large skillet over low heat. Add onion and garlic. Cook and stir 2 minutes, or until garlic is aromatic. Stir in molasses.
2. In a small bowl, mix powdered paprika, pepper, mustard, sugar and salt until smooth. Sprinkle seasoning blend over onions and garlic. Stir well. Add cider and tomato paste. Stir well and simmer 15 minutes. Add Worcestershire sauce to taste. If too thick, add a bit more cider.

Makes 2 cups.

Strong Cider BBQ Baste

Honey Ginger Ale Basting Sauce

This spicy baste adds moisture and flavor to pork chops that so often can dry out on the grill. Be careful to apply over indirect heat to avoid flare-ups.

- 2 cloves garlic, peeled and minced
- 2 tablespoons fresh grated ginger
- 1 tablespoon honey
- 1 teaspoon chili paste
- 2 tablespoons lime juice
- ⅛ teaspoon anise seeds
- ½ cup canola oil
- 1 cup honey ale

1. Place garlic, ginger, honey, chili paste, lime juice, anise seeds and canola oil in a large skillet over low heat. Cook and stir until garlic is tender, about 1 minute. Whisk in honey ale; simmer 5 minutes. Sauce will keep, covered in refrigerator, for up to 1 week.

Makes 1½ cups.

Brewer's Mop

Fred Bueltmann of New Holland Brewing Co., Holland, Michigan, uses the Sundog Amber ale for this mop recipe. I tweaked it to yield 3 cups, a generous amount for most barbecues. Fred says, "A straight forward mop to use during long, slow cooking times. When smoking brisket or pork shoulder, I hit it with the mop on the hour. It coats well, and brings in moisture and flavor, rather than caking up or burning like a sauce would."

- ¼ cup canola oil
- 1 cup minced onion
- 4 garlic cloves, peeled and minced (or more to taste)
- 12 ounces amber ale
- ½ cup cider vinegar
- ¼ cup water
- 2 tablespoons Worcestershire sauce
- 2 tablespoons Fred's Rub Mix (page 97)

1. Place oil and onion in a medium saucepan over low heat; cook and stir until onions are tender, and add garlic. Cook 1 minute. Add remaining ingredients and stir. Cook over medium heat for 15 minutes.

Makes 3 cups.

Hazelnut Brown Ale Mop

Good on grilled fish such as halibut. If you can't find a brown ale made with hazelnuts, such as the one made by Rogue Brewing Company of Oregon, use a brown ale and add 1 tablespoon hazelnut liqueur. You may also use prepared hazelnut butter, often sold at natural foods stores or in the health foods section of large grocery stores.

- ¼ teaspoon vanilla extract
- 4 ounces hazelnut brown ale
- 3 ounces hazelnut oil
- 2 tablespoons toasted and skinned hazelnuts
- ¼ cup minced chives
- ½ teaspoon salt
- ½ teaspoon ground black pepper

1. Place all ingredients in blender and purée on HIGH until smooth.

Makes 1 cup.

Browned Butter Dubbel Mop

- ½ cup butter (1 stick)
- 12 ounces strong dubbel ale, at room temperature
- 2 tablespoons Worcestershire sauce
- 2 to 3 tablespoons hot pepper sauce
- 1 tablespoon ground white pepper, or to taste

1. Place butter in heavy skillet over very low heat and simmer until milk solids turn golden brown, about 15 minutes. Let cool to lukewarm (should still be liquid) and skim off browned bits to make clarified butter (also known as ghee, an Indian staple ingredient).

2. Blend clarified butter in a blender on HIGH with all remaining ingredients. Use as a mop frequently while cooking ribs or pork loin.

Makes 1 ¾ cups.

Old Sourpuss Mop Sauce

The first time I tasted gueuze, I was startled by its sour taste. Here, it is mixed with vinegar in a mop sauce modeled after North Carolina barbecue. In Pennsylvania, Lancaster Brewing Co. makes an American gueuze called Old Sourpuss.

- 8 ounces gueuze or tart lambic ale
- 8 ounces apple cider vinegar
- 2 tablespoons butter
- 2 tablespoons ketchup
- 2 tablespoons grainy brown mustard
- 2 tablespoons dark brown sugar
- 1 tablespoon hot pepper sauce
- 1 teaspoon ground white pepper
- 1 teaspoon red pepper flakes
- 1 teaspoon salt

1. Mix all ingredients in a large nonreactive saucepan and bring to a simmer over low heat. Stir until butter melts and remove from heat. Use immediately on smoked pork shoulder.

Makes 2¼ cups.

Harpoon Championships of New England BBQ

The village of Windsor, site of the founding of the state of Vermont, is also home to the Harpoon Brewery's expanded brewhouse. Bought from the former Catamount Brewery, Harpoon's huge brewery and state-of-the-art bottling line, with gift shop and visitor's center, borders the Connecticut River.

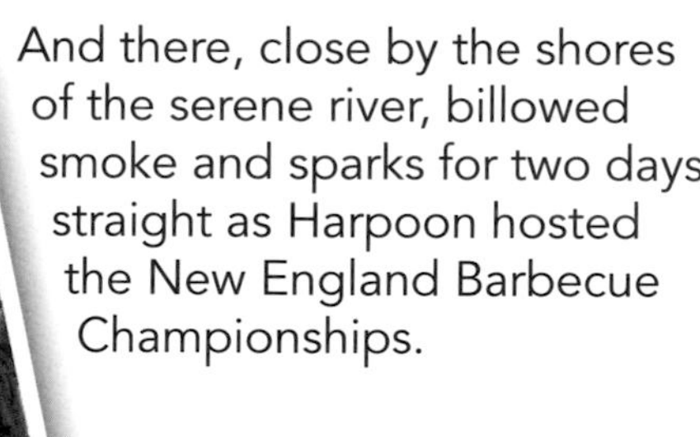

And there, close by the shores of the serene river, billowed smoke and sparks for two days straight as Harpoon hosted the New England Barbecue Championships.

More than 25 teams from across New England set up camp kitchens, built fires in BBQ pits, and pitched tents or spread sleeping bags in the back of their vans and trucks.

Overnight, shifts of cooks stoked their BBQ fires to stay "slow and low" for the most succulent ribs, briskets, and more.

Day two, the Championship BBQ judges sampled fare that required less lengthy tending, such as chicken wings, seafood, and the creative "chef's choice" category.

Throughout the weekend, the Harpoon Brewery poured beer and soda fresh from the brewery tanks. Brews on tap included the IPA, ESP, unfiltered hefeweizen UFO, and (new to me) the Harpoon Summer Beer—a truly tasty Kölsch ale.

Harpoon set up a sound stage providing music (The Nobby Reed Project, Dr. Burma, and Anything Goes), brewery tours and games (such as mini keg bowling) for the kids.

Led by Mark Gelo, officials certified by the Kansas City Barbecue Society judged four main categories: chicken, pork, ribs and brisket. Other categories included sausages and a special competition to make a BBQ dish with a beer-based sauce.

BBQ teams sported hilarious handles, such as Dr. Frank N Swine, Bare Bones, Pork Floyd, and I Smell Smoke!

The various pork memorabilia on display also gave fest-goers the giggles — a crowd favorite was the flying pig on display at the Smoke Ring of Cambridge. Chef Andy Husbands of Boston's Tremont 647 is a fan of Harpoon; his BBQ crew, Que BBQ, is sponsored by the brewery.

Husbands led the crew to victory in several categories. Their pulled pork shoulder was outstanding.

"We sold most of our samples by mid-day on Saturday," said Husbands.

"But I can't eat it anymore—by the time you've stayed up all night, drinking beer and tending the smoker, BBQ isn't high on the list."

Jamie Schier, a member of "Uncle Jed" LaBonte's crew, also works at Harpoon Brewery.

Schier stayed up all night with the crew, tending the pit for the brisket, which smoked for about 14 hours. Their team won several awards at the championships (Schier, pictured with his daughter, Ali, at right).

So much 'cue, so little time.

The pork ribs, pictured with a vibrant rub of paprika, cayenne and other spices, were

tender and juicy. "But I really like the Chef's Choice, which is a flank steak marinated overnight in Harpoon IPA, rice wine vinegar, ginger, cilantro and garlic—very simple, very delicious," says Schier.

"When you think about it, a flank steak really is like a mini brisket—it can take that tenderization from a long marinade."

After eating meat nonstop, it was refreshing to sample a yeasty flatbread that was grilled by the great cooks at King Arthur's Flour and Baking Center in nearby Norwich.

The bread was topped with minced garlic, a fabulous olive oil imported from Spain, and a bit of grated Vermont cheddar.

Outstanding. —L.S.

WWW.HARPOONBREWERY.COM

Grill Glazes

Pure speed is one of the reasons we love to grill—is there anything more nerve-wracking than knowing you can change a chop from juicy meat into something more like shoe leather in mere minutes? So, use glazes to add full-bodied flavors when every second counts.

Typically sweetened with brown sugar, malt syrup, fruit preserves or juices, honey, or molasses, glazes should be applied in the final 2 to 4 minutes of cooking. As a glaze caramelizes lightly on the food surface, it adds a sugary sheen and seasonings.

The difference between a grilling glaze and a barbecue sauce is that the latter is typically thicker and can be served as a condiment at the table. Glazes are more liquid in texture and often much sweeter. However, a barbecue sauce can be thinned with a splash of flavorful craft beer and do double-duty as a glaze. But after trying some of the fabulous recipes that follow, you'll understand why making a glaze is worth the time.

Apply caution and common sense along with a glaze—because it is thin and sugary, it can cause flare-ups. Avoid this by applying over low or indirect heat, or slide a swath of aluminum foil under your foods before painting on the glaze. Glazes keep for up to 2 weeks in the refrigerator if stored in glass or a nonreactive container with a tightly-fitted lid or seal.

Tamarind Amber Glaze

Tamarind paste is an ingredient commonly used in Indian recipes. You can find it in the ethnic foods section at large grocery stores, or by mail order (see Appendix II on page 206). If you can't find it, try making this glaze with 2 ounces dried apricots for a different, fruity flavor. Use as a glaze for pork, salmon or chicken.

- 2 ounces tamarind paste
- ½ cup water
- ½ cup unsweetened applesauce
- 8 ounces amber ale
- ¼ cup sesame oil
- 2 tablespoons hot paprika
- 2 tablespoons date sugar or molasses
- 1 teaspoon vanilla

1. Tamarind paste comes in blocks that look like black paste. To use, break off a 2-ounce chunk (about 3 inches) and place in small skillet with water. Cover and simmer over low heat, stirring occasionally to break up paste. Cook 10 minutes, cover, and set aside for 10 minutes.
2. In separate 1-quart saucepan, mix applesauce, ale, oil, paprika, date sugar and vanilla. Bring to a simmer over low heat. Add softened tamarind paste and pan juices. Cook and stir 5 minutes. Remove from heat and let cool to lukewarm. Press through a sieve with wooden spoon to remove stringy seeds from tamarind. Use as a glaze during final 5 minutes of grilling for pork, salmon or chicken.

Makes 2 cups.

Strawberry Honey Ale Glaze

If you buy strawberries in season and find some are too bruised or blemished to serve at the table, whip up a batch of this glaze. Use it as a glaze on grilled asparagus or swordfish.

- 1 cup very ripe strawberries, stemmed, coarsely chopped
- 1 teaspoon balsamic vinegar
- 1 tablespoon strawberry jam
- ½ cup honey ale
- ¼ cup walnut oil
- 1 tablespoon chopped fresh chives
- 1 teaspoon minced fresh tarragon
- 1 teaspoon lime juice
- ½ teaspoon salt
- ¼ teaspoon ground white pepper

1. Place strawberries in blender and sprinkle balsamic vinegar on top. Let stand 15 minutes. Add remaining ingredients to blender, cover and purée on HIGH until smooth.

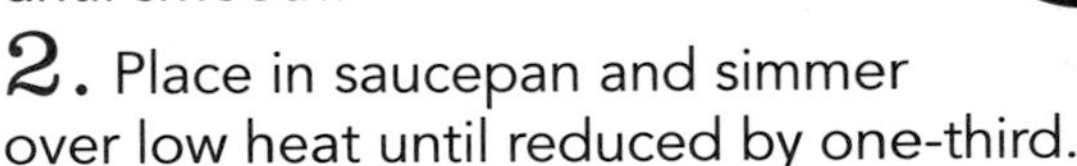

2. Place in saucepan and simmer over low heat until reduced by one-third.

Makes 1¼ cups.

Mustard Sage Glaze

Mustard Sage Glaze

- ½ cup prepared Dijon mustard
- 1 tablespoon minced fresh sage
- ½ cup amber ale
- 2 tablespoons melted butter
- 1 tablespoon molasses
- ½ teaspoon cracked black pepper

1. Whisk together all ingredients in medium bowl; brush on chops, steak or chicken or fish during last 5 minutes of cooking.

Makes 1 cup.

Smoky Porter Maple Glaze

A blend of smoked porter, maple syrup and barley malt syrup makes a sweet brown glaze for wild game or poultry. Smoked porters are popular in the West (Alaskan Brewing and Stone Brewing Co. both offer them), but imported German rauchbiers are also good. You can find malt syrup, also known as unhopped barley malt extract, at homebrew supply shops. Use the American Homebrewers Association website to find a homebrew supplier near you — www.beertown.org.

- ¼ cup maple syrup
- ¼ cup barley malt syrup
- 1 teaspoon fresh grated orange zest
- 2 teaspoons five-spice powder
- 1 tablespoon toasted sesame chili oil
- 4 ounces smoked porter or rauchbier

1. Place all ingredients in blender and purée on HIGH until smooth. Use immediately.

Makes 1 scant cup.

Sparkling Ale Fruit Grilling Glaze

Recipe by chef Eric Gillish of the Union Café, in Kalamazoo, Michigan. Gillish uses Bell's Sparkling Ale, a strong tripel-style ale, to make this glaze.

- ½ cup apple cider
- 12 ounces tripel-style ale
- 1 teaspoon grated orange zest
- ½ cup brown sugar
- ¼ teaspoon kosher salt
- Pinch white pepper

1. Place cider, sparkling ale and orange zest in a medium saucepan over medium-low heat, and simmer to reduce mixture to 1 cup. Remove from heat and strain.
2. Place strained mixture back in saucepan over medium heat, and add sugar, salt, and pinch of white pepper, whisking continuously until sugar dissolves. Remove from heat. Taste and adjust seasonings. Use as a glaze for grilled fish or fruits.

Makes 1½ cups.

A tripel earns its name from the extra stages of fermentation, and sometimes the exponential additions of malt, to make this strong ale, originally developed at a Trappist monastery. Craft brewers such as Bells's Brewery of Kalamazoo, Michigan and Jolly Pumpkin Artisan Ales of Dexter, Michigan, now make their own interpretations of tripels, often with Belgian "candi" sugar added for extra fermentable sugars.

Tripel Teriyaki Glaze

Chinese bead molasses is found in the Asian ethnic food sections at grocery stores. It is thicker and darker than blackstrap molasses.

- 12 ounces tripel ale
- ¼ cup roasted garlic purée
- 1 teaspoon grated ginger
- ¼ teaspoon Chinese mustard powder
- 2 teaspoons toasted sesame chili oil
- ½ cup soy sauce
- 2 tablespoons mirin (sweet rice wine)
- 2 tablespoons Chinese bead molasses

1. Mix all ingredients in medium saucepan and simmer over low heat, stirring occasionally, for 15 minutes. Use as a glaze on pork ribs, chicken wings, or shrimp.

Makes 1½ cups.

Sweet Cilantro Glaze

Try this on grilled shrimp or grilled Japanese eggplant.

- 4 ounces sweetened coconut milk
- 1 tablespoon Thai green curry paste (or more to taste)
- ½ cup chopped cilantro leaves
- ¼ cup minced green scallions (2 medium)
- ½ cup Asian lager

1. Place all ingredients in blender and purée on HIGH until smooth. Use immediately.

Makes 1⅓ cups.

Brown Shugga' Glaze

I made this recipe for the first time with Lagunitas Brewing Co.'s Brown Shugga' barley wine, but you could also make it with brown ale. It won't be quite as richly malty, but will still be delicious on grilled lamb or pork.

- 1 tablespoon butter
- ¼ cup brown sugar, packed
- 1 teaspoon ground ginger
- 1 teaspoon ground cinnamon
- 1 teaspoon ground black pepper
- 1 teaspoon garlic powder
- ½ teaspoon salt
- 3 ounces barley wine

1. Melt butter in small skillet over low heat. Add sugar, ginger, cinnamon, pepper, garlic powder and salt. Whisk until sugar dissolves. Mix in barley wine and brush on grilled lamb or pork.

Makes ½ cup.

Orange Chili Glaze

Excellent on appetizer-sized skewers of sliced pork tenderloin and chunks of bell pepper and pineapple.

- ½ cup orange marmalade
- 4 ounces Belgian dubbel or strong golden ale
- 1 tablespoon red chili paste
- ¼ teaspoon salt
- ¼ cup butter

1. Mix all ingredients in small saucepan placed over low heat. Cook and stir until marmalade melts, about 4 minutes. Use immediately.

Makes 1 cup.

Coconut Golden Ale Glaze

Tropical flavors for pork or chicken! You can also chop up cooked chicken or pork and stir it into the glaze before serving over rice or grilled plantains. Raw honey has a thicker texture than refined honey, but you may use the refined variety if raw honey is not available.

- 2 tablespoons grated ginger
- ½ cup minced shallots
- 1 tablespoon peanut oil
- 8 ounces strong golden ale
- 3 tablespoons tangerine juice
- 2 tablespoons raw honey
- Pinch salt
- 1 tablespoon coconut rum
- ¼ cup unsweetened finely grated dried coconut
- 1 teaspoon grated tangerine peel

1. Place ginger and shallots in 1-quart saucepan with peanut oil. Sauté over low heat until shallots are soft. Add ale, juice, honey, salt, rum, coconut and tangerine peel, stirring well.
2. Scrape mixture into blender and purée on HIGH until smooth. Return to saucepan and simmer 15 minutes. Apply while glaze is warm.

Makes 1¼ cups.

What kind of strong ale works in this recipe? An imported quadrupel such as Guldren Drak would complement these flavors. You could also try a strong ale aged in wood from breweries such as New Belgium Brewing Co. and Russian River Brewing Co.

Apple Ale Glaze

Use this glaze on grilled chicken or pork tenderloin.

- 1 tablespoon butter
- ½ cup minced onion
- ½ cup peeled and diced tart apple such as Granny Smith
- 1 tablespoon minced garlic
- 1 teaspoon grated ginger
- ½ teaspoon ground coriander
- 1 teaspoon ground turmeric, or to taste
- 1 tablespoon light brown sugar
- 1 teaspoon lemon juice
- 1 teaspoon salt
- ¼ teaspoon ground white pepper, or more to taste
- ¼ cup frozen apple juice concentrate
- 12 ounces pale ale

1. Melt butter in 2-quart saucepan. Add onion, apple and garlic. Cook and stir 2 minutes over medium-low heat. Add ginger, coriander, turmeric, light brown sugar, lemon juice, salt, white pepper and apple juice concentrate. Cook and stir 2 minutes. Remove from heat.

2. Let cool and place mixture in blender. Add pale ale and cover. Pulse on HIGH until mixture is emulsified. Return liquid to saucepan and simmer 15 minutes over very low heat, stirring often and being careful not to let mixture boil. It will separate if it boils; if this happens, remove from heat and place in blender with 1 tablespoon butter and purée until smooth.

Makes 2¼ cups.

Extra Special Teriyaki Sauce

Jill Ramiel of the Silverbow Inn in Juneau, Alaska, shares her recipe for teriyaki sauce made with Alaskan Brewery's Extra Special Bitter ale.

- 2 cups soy sauce
- ⅜ cup honey
- ⅜ white wine
- ¾ cup red wine vinegar
- 1 cup sugar
- 2 tablespoons ground ginger
- 12 ounces ESB (extra special bitter) ale

1. Place all ingredients in a large saucepan over medium-high heat, and stir. Bring to a simmering boil, reduce heat to LOW, and let the mixture reduce by half. Stir often to prevent sugar from scorching. Remove from heat and let cool. Excellent over ribs or fish.

Makes 2½ cups.

Tractor Brewing Rolls Into Pork and Brew

by Anne Ausderau

Editor, Southwest Brewing News

Wouldn't you like to spend two days outdoors, cooking meat on a smokin' grill? Add to that a smooth microbrewed red ale in your hand. Throw in a day of camaraderie and the aroma of hickory and mesquite wood chips swarming all around.

But wait—every 30 minutes an entry is due to the judges. Did the chile flavor come through in the salsa? Was the chicken cooked to perfection? Were the ribs plated properly? Was the right amount of sauce slathered on the brisket? Were the beans spicy enough?

That's what brewchef Ethan Diness and co-captain Hillary Dawson hoped. They participated in one smoky competition as fans of craft brewers and good barbecue. Entering as the "Mule Kickin' Beer-B-Q Crew," they entered

several categories of meats, sides and desserts. Okay, maybe it wasn't relaxing, but it was fun.

Thirty-three teams competed in the 1st Annual New Mexico Pork & Brew State Championship in Rio Rancho in 2004, which is now held each March as a Kansas City Barbecue Society sanctioned event. The Grand Champion qualifies to enter the American Royal Invitational held in Kansas City in late September.

One of the Mule Kickin' team's entries was their Fire Truck Stout Sauce—the "meanest mule of them all." Prepared with smoked chipotle peppers made from jalapeños grown in Albuquerque's north valley dolloped with stout, this one definitely kicked.

Diness explained the mule theme simply, "The mule was the first tractor." The Tractor mule team intended to do some serious kickin' in the contest.

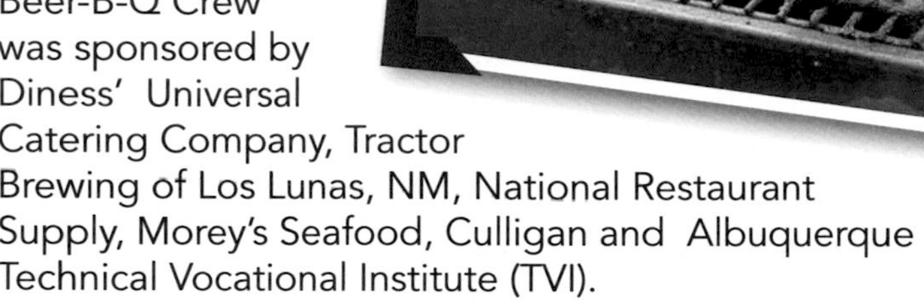

And all of his dishes had one of Tractor's brews as an important ingredient, plus the equivalent kick of a mule, from added chiles, herbs, and spices.

The Mule Kickin' Beer-B-Q Crew was sponsored by Diness' Universal Catering Company, Tractor Brewing of Los Lunas, NM, National Restaurant Supply, Morey's Seafood, Culligan and Albuquerque Technical Vocational Institute (TVI).

Diness and Dawson are both students in TVI's culinary arts division. Diness is also a part-time instructor in the program. Among his many specialties are Pacific Rim dishes and smoked meats, while Dawson's are pastries and sculpted sweet baked products. That accounts for the whimsical cakes sitting on the table that seemed to attract kids of all ages. The two most fanciful were a large pink pig and a John Deere tractor.

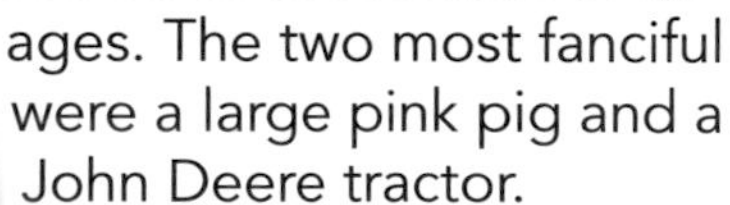

The only glitch on these days filled with food, old and new friends and good times was one of the main sponsors. It was Anheuser-Busch's brand, Budweiser. That's right—great barbecue, live entertainment, carnival rides and barely (not barley) flavored beer. So even though Diness had several growlers on ice filled with tasty Tractor craft brews, he wasn't allowed to sell any, give any away (except to lucky team members) or let anyone else enjoy it—except the judges when tasting it in his culinary creations.

The Mule Kickin' Beer-B-Q Crew ended up winning 8th place in the miscellaneous division for their salmon marinated in Tractor Haymaker Honey Wheat and 10th place in the desserts division for the piggy-wiggy cake. Not too shabby for their first try, and very well done when you consider many of the entrants do nothing but enter these competitions. It was also a great learning experience for this crew.

Now, if the organizers of the barbecue competition would serve the region's fine craft brews alongside the sponsor's brands, it would truly turn up the heat.

2005 copyright
www.brewingnews.com
Reprinted by permission of
www.brewingnews.com

Photos Brian Ausderau
Text by Anne Ausderau

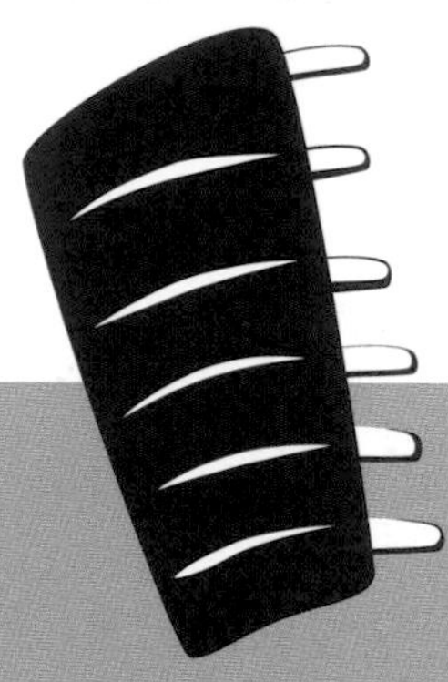

Ribs & Rubs

Why use a spice rub? If you don't have time to marinate or brine your grilled foods, rub on spices for an extra layer of flavor. A good spice rub or paste will add a toothsome crust, golden-brown color, and aroma to even the palest lobes of boned pork. And on slow-cooked meats such as ribs, a spice rub seals in juices and caramelizes the exterior of the meat.

Both salt and sugar are usually added to spices to make a rub, but I often omit the sugar if I am grilling over an open flame or uncontrolled high heat to prevent charring or flare-ups. If used correctly, a spice rub should help prevent food from sticking to the grill.

You can make a wet paste to brush on your "rub" if you don't like the idea of using your fingers to massage raw meat or poultry. Just blend in a mixture of equal parts beer and oil until the spice rub becomes thick and pasty. For the squeamish, I recommend putting on a pair of disposable latex gloves to rub on spices, or placing the rub in a plastic bag along with the foods to be grilled, and pressing the rub onto the surface through the plastic. Sometimes, I will spritz the surface of the grilled foods with nonstick cooking spray before dusting them with the spice rub blend. The light coating of oil keeps the food moist, as does basting with beer. Keep a spray bottle filled with fresh lager by the grill to control flare-ups and add flavor to the food as well.

beerbistro Apple Ale Ribs

Chef Brian Morin of beerbistro in Toronto, Ontario, Canada shares this recipe, created with Unibroue's Éphémère Pomme (apple ale). If apple ale is unavailable, try it with hard or strong cider.

- 6 baby back pork ribs (about 12 pounds)
- 1½ lemons, cut into slices
- 2 onions, chopped
- 2 teaspoons black peppercorns
- 3 bottles apple ale
- ¼ cup rib rub (recipe on p. 88)
- 2 cups Apple Ale Barbeque Sauce (recipe on p. 88)

1. Preheat oven to 310°F. Peel off white membrane underneath ribs. Place ribs in a roasting pan, stand ribs "spine-side down" and arrange "meat to meat" and "membrane side to membrane side" to allow space between slabs. Distribute cut lemons, chopped onion and black peppercorn over ribs. Pour apple ale over ribs in roasting pan so that ribs are almost covered in beer. Place a lid over roasting pan or cover tightly with aluminum foil.

2. Transfer roasting pan to oven and allow 3 hours to cook. Uncover one side of roasting pan. Test for "doneness." Use a fork to pierce meat between bones. Twist fork. If bones do not separate easily, reseal and cook for an additional 15 to 20 minutes. Recheck for doneness and repeat if necessary until meat is tender. When ribs are done, remove from oven and let cool in beer to absorb liquid. Once cool, remove and store for later use.

3. When ready to eat, heat ribs on grill, dust with rib rub and heat until rub caramelizes. Baste with barbeque sauce and allow sauce to caramelize and dry onto ribs. Serve at once.

Makes 8 to 12 servings.

beerbistro
Apple Ale Ribs

Morin's Rib Rub

- 1 pound granulated sugar
- 10 ounces (weight) salt
- 6 ounces (weight) ground paprika
- 2 ounces (weight) ground black pepper
- 3 ounces (weight) granulated garlic
- 1½ ounces (weight) cumin
- 1 ounce (weight) powdered mustard
- 1 ounce (weight) onion powder
- 1 ounce (weight) chili powder
- ¼ ounce (weight) ground cayenne to taste

1. Mix all ingredients and use as a rub for beerbistro Apple Ale Ribs (page 86).

Makes 2 pounds spice rub.

Apple Ale Barbeque Sauce

- 2 tablespoons butter
- 2 cups diced onion
- ½ cup apple cider vinegar
- 3 cups apple ale
- Zest and juice of one half lemon
- 4 cups ketchup

1. Place all ingredients into large heavy-bottomed pot, bring to a boil and reduce by almost one-half, until sauce coats back of wooden spoon. Strain through fine strainer.

Makes 1 scant quart.

IPA Spice Paste

- ½ cup minced onion
- ¼ cup walnut oil
- ¼ cup IPA
- ⅓ cup fresh cilantro, chopped
- ⅓ cup fresh parsley, chopped
- 2 tablespoons minced garlic
- 1 tablespoon paprika
- 1 tablespoon cinnamon
- 1 tablespoon grated orange zest
- 2 teaspoons salt (kosher)
- 1 teaspoon cumin

1. Place all ingredients in a food processor fitted with the metal cutting blade. Pulse on HIGH until pasty. Rub on chicken or lamb chops.

Makes about 1½ cups.

Randy's Spice Rub and BBQ Base

When I invited homebrewer Randy Mosher to contribute a spice rub recipe to this book, he shared more than a single recipe: he shared an entire system for creating seasoning blends customized to taste.

"The idea behind this is that there is a Master Spice Rub (p. 92) that can then be used in a dry rub, brine/marinade and table sauce," says Mosher. "This is a very loose recipe, and much variation is possible. I usually add lots of offbeat ethnic ingredients like grains of paradise, usuza seed, ajwan and galangal. Anything with a burn, a tingle, or a deeply spicy aroma is suitable."

If you don't have access to ethnic foods locally, shop online for these spices at www.spicehouse.com. The Spice House of Milwaukee has been supplying homebrewers since 1985, and even has their own blend of barbecue spices. Likewise, Vann's Spices, www.vanns.com, has worked with the National Barbecue Association for more than 20 years.

Randy's Rib Rub

- ½ cup Mosher's Master Spice Rub (p. 92)
- 1 tablespoon kosher or fine ground sea salt
- 1 cup brown sugar
- ¼ cup black pepper
- ¼ cup onion powder
- 1 tablespoon garlic powder

1. Mix all ingredients and use as rub for pork or beef ribs.

Makes 2 cups.

Randy's Seasoned Rub

"With herby-savory characteristics, this rub is a pretty good base seasoning for everything from salmon to steak," says Randy.

- 1 tablespoon toasted onion powder
- 1 tablespoon whole coriander
- 20 to 30 bay leaves
- 1 teaspoon rosemary
- 2 teaspoons marjoram
- 2 teaspoons Mexican oregano
- 2 teaspoons Greek oregano
- 1 teaspoon celery seed

1. Grind all whole ingredients in coffee mill to medium powder, and mix with pre-ground ingredients. Sprinkle on meat before grilling or smoking.

The Spice House of Evanston, Illinois and Milwaukee, Wisconsin, offers a toasted onion powder that tastes caramelized like French onion soup, and much fresher and lower in sodium than a dry onion soup mix (see p. 209 for mail order details).

Mosher's Master Spice Rub

- ½ teaspoon whole allspice
- ½ cup whole black peppercorns
- 1 teaspoon caraway seed
- 1 tablespoon celery seed
- 1 cup ancho chile
- ½ cup guajillo chile
- 1 teaspoon ground cinnamon
- 2 teaspoons plain unsweetened cocoa powder
- 2 tablespoons coriander seed
- ¼ cup garlic powder, toasted
- 1 tablespoon powdered ginger
- 1 tablespoon mustard powder
- ¼ teaspoon ground nutmeg
- ½ cup onion powder, toasted
- 1 tablespoon ground Mexican oregano
- ½ teaspoon star anise, powdered
- 1 teaspoon thyme

1. Grind all non-powdered ingredients in a coffee grinder, then blend all together. Store in an air-tight container. Non-toasted onion and garlic powder may be substituted for toasted, but the flavor will not be identical.

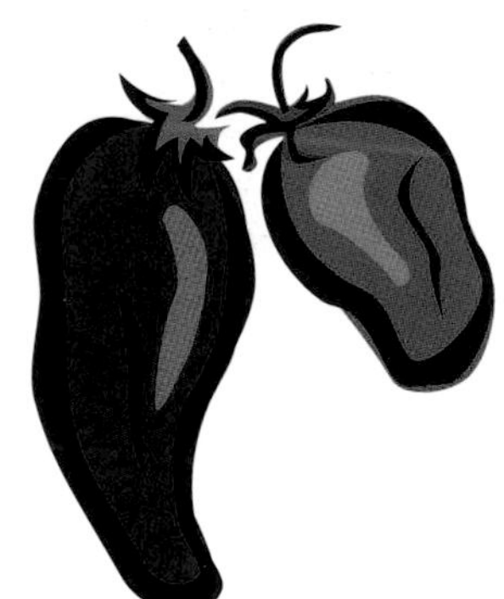

Makes about 4 cups.

Mosher's Mop BBQ sauce

- 2 cups ketchup
- 1 cup molasses
- ¼ cup cider vinegar or lemon juice
- ¼ cup dark ale
- 2 tablespoons (or more) Mosher's Master Spice Rub (recipe on p. 92)

1. Mix all ingredients and use on grilled beef or pork. For lighter dishes like chicken, honey or corn syrup may be substituted for part or all of the molasses.

Makes about 2½ cups.

> Note: Mosher likes to use ethnic sugars like panela (Latin) or gula jawa (Indonesian palm sugar), as he finds these have a cleaner sweet flavor, and a more interesting and exotic character compared to molasses. "These need to be broken up and simmered with the other ingredients to dissolve," he says, adding, "A splash of bourbon or rum at the end is usually welcome."

Malty Spice Rub

- 1 tablespoon powdered dark barley malt
- 2 tablespoons dark brown sugar
- 2 tablespoons hot paprika
- 1 tablespoon ground ancho chile
- 1 tablespoon onion powder
- 2 teaspoons cumin
- 2 tablespoons kosher salt
- 1 teaspoon ground allspice
- 2 tablespoons brown mustard seeds
- 1 to 2 tablespoons cracked black pepper

1. Mix all ingredients well and use as a rub for beef or pork.

Makes just over ¾ cup.

Tip: Visit beertown.org, the American Homebrewers Association website, to find a home brew store or supplier for the dark roasted malted barley. Just grind the grains into a powder in a coffee grinder. Don't substitute a barley drink mix.

Malty Spice Rub

Barley Wine BBQ Pork

A searing sauce using a strong ale or winter warmer, best served over pork ribs or pork shoulder.

- ¼ cup minced garlic
- 1 cup chopped white onion
- ¼ cup minced scallion (green leaves)
- 2 to 3 habañero or Scotch bonnet chiles, or more to taste, seeded and minced
- ¼ cup butter
- 1 tablespoon Asian five-spice powder
- 1 tablespoon cracked black pepper
- 1 tablespoon dried thyme
- 1 teaspoon ground allspice
- 1 teaspoon ground nutmeg
- 2 tablespoons fresh lime juice
- ¼ cup soy sauce
- 12 ounces barley wine (winter spiced seasonal is OK)
- 3 pounds pork shoulder

1. Place garlic, onion, scallion, chiles and butter in medium skillet and cook and stir over medium heat until onion is tender. Scrape mixture into blender and add all remaining ingredients; set aside skillet and do not clean. Cover and puree on HIGH until smooth. Return mixture to skillet and simmer 15 minutes to meld flavors. Reserve ½ cup mixture for basting.

2. Marinate 2 to 3 lbs. pork shoulder overnight in remaining barley wine BBQ mixture. Prepare grill with wood chips or smoker, and smoke pork over low heat for several hours, or until tender. Brush pork with reserved beer mixture several times each hour. The pork's internal temperature should reach 165°F. Although some food scientists recommend cooking to 190°F, I find the higher temperature makes the meat dry.

Pull apart pork using 2 forks and remove excess fat and gristle. Serve pulled pork warm over rice with Brewer's Mustard Coleslaw (page 167).

Makes 4 to 6 servings

Fred's Rub Mix

- ½ cup ground black pepper
- ½ cup paprika
- 1 cup turbinado sugar
- ¼ cup finely ground sea salt
- 1 tablespoon ground mustard
- 2 tablespoons onion powder
- ½ teaspoon cayenne powder (or more to taste)

1. Combine all ingredients in a re-sealable glass jar. Cover and shake.

Makes 2½ cups

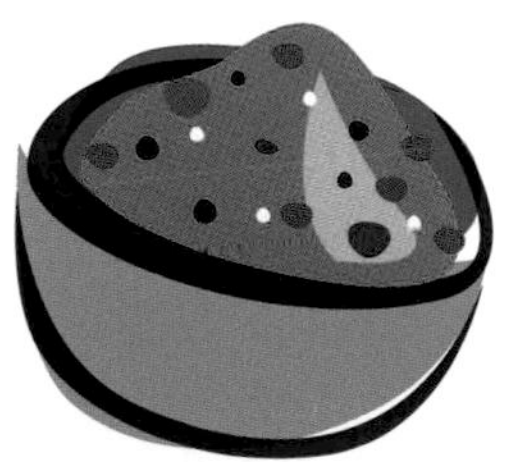

Leff's Stout Smoked Ribs

Dan Leff lives in California and has worked at the Lark Creek Inn. He enjoys West Coast craft brews and offers this recipe for Stout Smoked Pork Ribs:

- 1 rack pork ribs
- 2 tablespoons kosher salt
- 1 tablespoon cayenne pepper
- 1 tablespoon ground black pepper
- 2 tablespoons dark brown sugar
- 24 ounces stout
- 2 to 4 whole dried chiles (try mixing pasilla, aji limones, de Arbol, and chipotles)
- 2 cups apple cider
- ¼ to ½ cup soy sauce, to taste
- 1 quart apple juice
- ½ cup calvados (apple brandy)
- 1 small can (5 ounces) tomato paste
- 2 tablespoons chipotles en adobo

Gear:

Mesquite charcoal and apple wood smoking chips (about 2 cups)

Disposable aluminum baking pan (8x6x1½-inches)

1. Remove membrane from ribs. Mix kosher salt, cayenne pepper, ground black pepper and brown sugar. Rub pork ribs with mixture and place in large glass or stainless steel bowl. Set aside at room temperature for 30 minutes to dry.

2. Mix stout, chiles, cider and soy sauce. Pour over ribs, cover and chill overnight, or at least 4 hours.

3. Soak apple wood chips in apple juice and calvados. Allow to soak for same amount of time as ribs (minimum 4 hours, overnight is best).

4. Remove pork from refrigerator and let sit for 1 to 2 hours while preparing fire. Prepare a charcoal fire: when coals ash over, separate coals (using small garden hoe or long-handled offset spatula) into 2 piles, each pushed to one side of bottom of grill, with room for baking pan in between. (Note: Don't try to start with 2 separate piles and try to light them separately—they'll never ash over at an even rate.)

5. Drain apple-calvados mixture from wood chips into a pitcher or bowl with spout. Reserve soaking liquid. Drain stout mixture from ribs, and transfer to a medium saucepan. Set aside.

6. Position baking pan squarely in between hot coals. Immediately pour in soaking liquid from apple wood chips. Sprinkle chips evenly over both piles of coals, then place the grilling rack on grill top.

7. Place ribs on grill grate, directly over baking pan so fat drips into pan. Allow a few minutes for wood chips to start smoking, then close grill cover and open vents.

8. Ribs will take about 2 hours to cook. Lid may need to be removed every 30 minutes to allow coals to start smoking again if fire starts dying down. Turn ribs every 30 minutes. While ribs are cooking; heat marinade in shallow pan over medium heat. When the mixture comes to a boil, stir in tomato paste. Reduce heat and simmer until thickened. Add chipotles en adobo. This will be table sauce for ribs. Ribs are done when tender; serve with sauce.

Makes 8 servings.

Australian Craft Beer & the Barby

"When an American refers to "shrimp on the barbie," it makes me smile," Master Brewer Bill Taylor arched his eyebrows, and explained as he passed a platter of pancetta-wrapped, stout-glazed grilled crustaceans, "because around here, we call them *prawns.*"

So, look beyond stereotypes when exploring Australian food and beer. Australian beer is more than just plain " gold and cold," as craft breweries, from Blue Tongue to Little Creatures to Redoak, offer creative beer styles from bock to stout.

Pioneering brewers, such as Chuck Hahn of the Malt Shovel Brewery and Bill Taylor of its parent company, Lion-Nathan, and chefs such as John Meredith of Brisbane and Aaron Ross of Sydney, pave the way for pairing barbecue and brews with vastly more flavor and complexity.

John Meredith of the James St. Cooking School, caterer to rock fests such as Big Day Out and exuberant chef, brings craft beer to the grilling crowd through popular "Beer and Barbeque" classes. Brewers Chuck Hahn and Bill Taylor often sample their brands at Meredith's class.

Meredith, at left, believes that "cooking should use all your senses, so that tasting, touching, smelling ingredients, seeing how the dish is made, all helps you to appreciate the flavors." Many of the ingredients are sold at the James St. Market, one of the best fresh markets in Brisbane.

Lots of couples enrolled in the "Beer and Barbeque" class, plus myself and a few other single students. All of us taste the Squires line of brews, and quiz Meredith for tips on grilling and entertaining. "Planning a party around grilled food is so easy," says Meredith, "because you can cook appetizers on skewers and serve straight from the grill."

Another popular destination for beer and barby in Brisbane is The Breakfast Creek Hotel, nicknamed the "Brekky Creek." Topped with an ancient XXXX Castlemaine sign that turned the building into an historic landmark, the hotel is famous for its barbecue and lager served from a wooden keg.

Though the lager is not fermented in the wood, the Hotel staff do keep up with the labor of conditioning the wood barrels and keeping them cool and clean to serve lager. A keg of Castlemaine "Fourex" lager ages about a week in the wood before being hoisted to the Brekky bar for tapping. A cask is ceremoniously tapped every day at 5 PM, most refreshing when paired with spicy shrimp and a grilled steak from the barbecue.

After studying up in Brisbane, I traveled to Sydney for a tasting of grilled foods at the Wharf Restaurant. The BBQ was paired and prepared with the James Squire line of beers from the Malt Shovel Brewery, and Southwark brews from Lion-Nathan. Chuck Hahn and Bill Taylor (pictured at left with chef Aaron Ross) hosted the event for food writers interested in craft beer, including Carol Selva Rajah, who is also a frequent guest teacher at the James St. Cooking School.

"Asian and Indian ingredients harmonize with the flavors of beer," says spokesperson Selva Rajah. "There is a natural synergy of beer and spices, and together their flavors produce layers of deliciously subtle interactions." She specially likes aromatic curry spices like cumin and fenugreek with yeasty, bitter ales such as IPA.

Our BBQ feast began with pancetta-wrapped prawns grilled with Southwark Stout and served

with Hahn premium lager, spicy ale-brined BBQ chicken with James Squire Amber Ale, and TropicAle Pork Chops (page 182) served with James Squire Golden Ale. Chef Ross made a sweet Barley Wort Sorbet with White Peaches, served with the contrasting roasted flavors of James Squire Porter.

"The barbecue exemplifies the important role of beer in Australian eating," says Taylor in his book, BEER AND FOOD: A Celebration of Flavours (Beckett Maynard Publishing, 2002). "Everybody loves a good barbie, from the heady smell of char-grilled meats…to the bracing taste of a flavorful beer."

Sydney is both casual and cosmopolitan, so craft beer can be found tableside at dozens of waterfront bistros, cafes and restaurants dotting the harbors of the city.

But in Australia, as in the U.S., "there are more craft brews with varied flavors and styles that harmonize with food." Says Peter Lee, editor of bbqblue.com.au, "That is precisely why there has been such a surge in sales of boutique beers."

Lee adds that no discussion of Australian beer is complete without mentioning Coopers. This South Australian brewery has been family owned since 1862 and maintains its independence. Coopers, crisp and malty, is delightful with seafood, shown paired with a grilled oyster at the Catalina Restaurant. Truly a classic match!
—L.S.

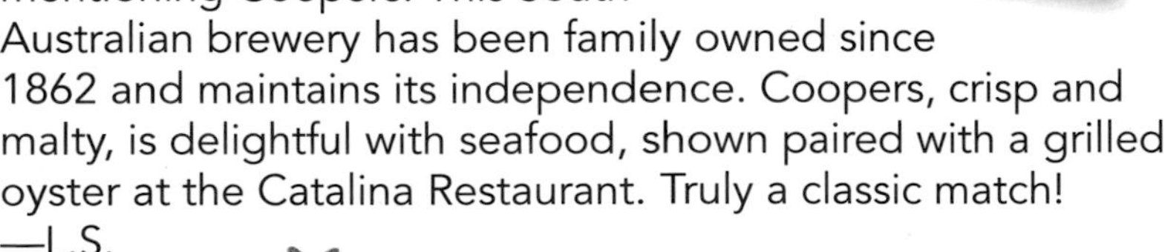

Malty Marinades & Brines

Look closely at almost any meat label in a supermarket or grocery, and in small type you'll find a percentage. That figure represents the percent of tumbling solution added, injected, or "tumbled" with the meat. Why do meat processors do this? Salt in the solution adds shelf life, and the water weight adds to the total weight of the package. This means that a "tumbled" product may be tender and pre-brined, but also costs more per pound for the consumer!

But the solution isn't composed merely of water and plain salt. Many additives go into commercial meat tumbling solutions, from calcium fluoroapatite phosphates, hydrocolloid carrageenans, amylose, amylose pectin, dextrins, and other starches.[1]

Seek out butcher shops or natural foods stores that offer meats and poultry that have not been "tumbled." Some meat merchants, such as the Niman Ranch Co., will even ship to your door. Add your own marinades and brines made with craft beer to bring better flavor to the table. Many of these marinades taste wonderful with grilled vegetables such as sweet onions, plantains and eggplant.

1 Source, Foster, R.J., "Meating Consumer Expectations." *Food Product Design*, Virgo Publishing (December 2004).

Mojo Malt Marinade

- 1 banana pepper, seeded and minced
- 1 teaspoon ground cumin
- 2 tablespoons minced garlic
- 1 tablespoon canola oil
- 12 ounces Mexican dark lager
- ½ cup chopped cilantro
- ¼ cup lime juice

1. Mix pepper, cumin and garlic in small saucepan with canola oil. Cook over low heat, stirring often, 5 minutes.

2. Remove from heat and cool. Place in blender with lager, cilantro and lime juice. Blend on HIGH until smooth.

Makes 2 cups.

Barley Malt Brine

A simple brine that adds lots of toasty ale taste and caramel color to grilled meats and poultry. Barley malt extract or syrup is an alternative sweetener often found at natural food stores. You can buy it online from Eden Foods *(see Appendix II, page 208).*

- 12 ounces porter
- ¼ cup barley malt extract
- ¼ cup malt vinegar
- ¼ cup packed brown sugar
- ⅓ cup kosher salt
- 1 teaspoon freshly ground black pepper
- 1 clove garlic, peeled

1. Place all ingredients in blender and mix on HIGH until emulsified. Place in resealable plastic bag with meat or poultry to be brined.

Makes 1½ cups.

Hazelnut Maibock Marinade

Although the flavor is nutty and delicious, this marinade looks a bit ashen on the grill top. Use as a marinade for pork or lamb, or as a basting sauce for grilled squash or peppers and garnish with minced scallions and grated lemon zest.

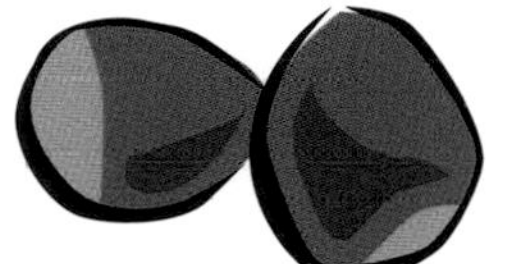

- 2 ounces chopped shallots
- 2 tablespoons hazelnut oil
- ⅓ cup toasted chopped hazelnuts
- 1 ounce hazelnut liqueur
- 12 ounces maibock or strong golden ale
- ¼ teaspoon lemon zest
- 1 clove garlic, peeled and minced
- ⅛ teaspoon allspice
- ⅛ teaspoon white pepper
- ¼ cup raw honey

1. Place shallots, oil and hazelnuts in 1-quart saucepan; sauté over low heat until shallots are tender. Add remaining ingredients and cook and stir 10 minutes.

2. Remove from heat, scrape mixture into blender, and blend on HIGH until creamy.

Makes 1¾ cups.

Safety tip: Cover blender lid with a folded tea towel and hold lid in place when mixing warm liquids. The heat generates steam that may expand and push off the blender lid. Hold lid in place firmly during operation.

Porter Lime Mustard Marinade

Try this on baby lamb chops, as Beer Chef Bruce Paton did at a tasting we held at the Cathedral Hill Hotel in San Francisco, California.

- 12 ounces porter
- ¼ cup toasted sesame oil
- 2 tablespoons lime juice
- 1 teaspoon grated lime zest
- ½ teaspoon powdered ginger, or more to taste
- ½ teaspoon freshly ground black pepper, or more to taste
- ⅓ cup grainy mustard OR ¼ cup Dijon mustard and 1 tablespoon brown mustard seeds

1. Mix all ingredients in blender on HIGH until emulsified. Use as a marinade for lamb or beef.

Makes 1½ cups.

White Balsamic-Witbier Marinade

Raw honey is not filtered, so it is almost creamy in texture. Because it is thicker than refined honey, it adds body to the marinade and has a richer, mellower flavor that offsets the witbier well. Filtered honey may be substituted, but the taste and texture will be different.

- 12 ounces witbier
- ¼ cup white balsamic vinegar
- ¼ cup sesame oil
- 1 teaspoon kosher salt
- ¼ teaspoon pink peppercorns
- ¼ cup raw honey
- 1 tablespoon crushed bay leaves
- ⅛ teaspoon ground cardamom

1. Mix all ingredients in blender on HIGH. Use as marinade for salmon or boneless skinless chicken breasts. Marinate at least 2 hours for best flavor.

Makes 2 cups.

Dunkel Weiss & Spice Marinade

Dunkel Weiss & Spice Marinade

"My new favorite for steak," says recipe tester Shaun. "It lets the flavor of the meat come through, but adds lots of spice." You may also simmer the marinade and add 1 teaspoon cornstarch mixed with 1 tablespoon cold water to make a slurry to thicken it. The thickened sauce may be used to plate the final dish. Good on steak, chops and turkey breast.

- 1 teaspoon fennel seed
- 1 teaspoon black mustard seeds
- ¼ teaspoon celery seeds
- 1 teaspoon red pepper flakes, or more to taste
- 3 cloves garlic, peeled and chopped
- ½ teaspoon kosher salt
- ½ teaspoon ground chipotle pepper
- 1 tablespoon dark brown sugar
- ¼ cup canola oil
- 12 ounces dunkel weiss or black wheat ale

1. Toast fennel, mustard and celery seeds in a heavy skillet over medium heat until mustard seeds start to pop. Remove from heat and scrape into blender container.

2. Add all remaining ingredients. Cover blender and blend on HIGH until smooth.

Makes 1½ cups.

Cajun Herb Marinade

- 2 tablespoons Cajun spice blend
- 1 tablespoon Worcestershire sauce
- 2 teaspoons minced fresh rosemary
- 2 tablespoons minced fresh parsley
- 2 tablespoons minced fresh green onion
- 1 tablespoon minced garlic
- 1 tablespoon ground paprika
- 8 ounces hoppy amber ale
- 4 ounces canola oil

1. Blend all ingredients in a blender on HIGH until smooth. Use as a marinade for seafood or chicken tenders.

Makes 1½ cups.

Imperial Stout Marinade

Chef Bruce Paton's beer dinners at the Cathedral Hill Hotel in San Francisco draw hundreds of diners to celebrate the brewing community in California. This simple marinade packs enormous flavor and may be used on pork or beef.

- 1 cup Imperial stout
- ½ cup chopped garlic
- ¼ cup pimenton dulce (sweet smoked paprika)
- ¼ cup coarse grainy Dijon mustard
- 1 cup olive oil

1. Combine all ingredients and use as marinade for pork or beef, for at least 4 hours or overnight.

Makes 2½ cups.

Flying Fish Horseradish Marinade

Gene Muller, brewer and owner of Flying Fish Brewery in New Jersey, enjoys grilling and cooking. He makes the following marinade with his brewery's Belgian-style Dubbel, and uses it on beef brisket and flank steaks.

- 24 ounces dubbel
- ½ cup olive oil
- 1 tablespoon red wine vinegar
- 2 teaspoons finely minced garlic
- 2 teaspoons salt
- 1 teaspoon ground cayenne pepper
- 1 tablespoon prepared horseradish (or more to taste)
- 2 tablespoons lemon juice

1. Mix all ingredients together; reserve ⅓ cup to use as a basting sauce while grilling.

Makes enough to marinate 2 to 3 pounds beef.

Belgian Ale Marinade

Steven Raichlen, award-winning author and host of Barbecue University, shares this recipe from the Barbecue! Bible Sauces, Rubs and Marinades ($12.95, Workman Publishing). Steve says, "Barbecue without beer would be like, well, life without breathing. Beer is the beverage of choice among most of the world's barbecue cultures," and it's an essential ingredient in this recipe.

- 2 cups Belgian-style golden ale
- ¼ cup honey mustard
- ¼ cup canola oil
- 1 teaspoon coarse sea salt
- 1 teaspoon freshly ground black pepper
- 1 medium onion, peeled and thinly sliced
- ½ green or red bell pepper, stemmed, seeded and finely chopped
- 4 scallions, trimmed and chopped (include white and green parts)
- 4 cloves garlic, peeled and smashed
- 2 slices fresh ginger (each ¼ inch thick), peeled and smashed
- 1 tablespoon pickling spice
- 1 tablespoon paprika
- ½ teaspoon caraway seeds

1. Combine the ale, mustard, oil, salt and pepper in a nonreactive mixing bowl. Stir or whisk until salt is dissolved. Add the remaining ingredients and stir. Pour mixture into a large glass jar fitted with a lid, cover and refrigerate. The marinade will keep for up to 3 days.

Makes 2½ cups.

Lemon Weiss Marinade

Lew Bryson, author of beer and pub travel guides, tells me that he's not an organized chef, but still "likes to throw chicken on the grill" after a soak in this marinade.

- Juice of 1 lemon (about ¼ cup)
- 12 ounces weissbier
- Pinch ground cumin
- 1 teaspoon freshly ground black pepper
- 1 cup minced onion
- ¼ cup canola oil

1. Mix all ingredients in a large nonreactive bowl. Use to marinate chicken (also good on fish).

Makes 2 cups.

Tarragon IPA Brine

Emily, one of the champion recipe testers for this book, especially liked the blend of tarragon and pungent oil-cured olives. Don't substitute plain canned black or green ripe olives, as the flavor will change completely. Use this brine on lamb, poultry, or eggplant for at least 2 hours for best flavor.

- 12 ounces hoppy IPA
- ¼ cup chopped fresh tarragon
- ¼ cup oil-cured black olives, pitted and chopped
- 2 tablespoons balsamic vinegar
- 1 teaspoon white pepper
- 2 tablespoons buckwheat honey or dark cane syrup
- 2 tablespoons kosher salt

1. Blend all ingredients in a blender on HIGH until mixed well. Use as brine or marinade.

2. If using brine on vegetables such as eggplant or portobello mushrooms, mixture may be reused in grilling. Pour reserved brine through a mesh sieve to remove herb-olive solids, and apply as a paste on vegetables before cooking.

Makes 1¾ cups.

Amber Ale Madras Marinade

- 1 teaspoon cumin seeds
- 2 teaspoons brown mustard seeds
- 2 tablespoons vegetable oil
- 1 teaspoon hot Madras curry powder
- 1 clove fresh minced garlic (about ½ teaspoon)
- ½ cup chopped onion
- 1 bottle (12 ounces) fruity amber ale
- Salt and freshly ground pepper, to taste
- 2 tablespoons chopped fresh Italian parsley

1. Place seeds and vegetable oil in small skillet over low heat and toast seeds. Remove from heat and place in blender with remaining ingredients. Purée on HIGH until emulsified.

Makes 1¾ cups.

Blues, Brews and Barbecue Festival at Beaver Creek

Story by Dan Rabin

Photos by Dan & Karen Rabin

It may be coincidence that three of life's great pleasures - beer, blues and barbecue – all begin with the letter "B." But when one of Colorado's most posh mountain resorts offers up this alliteration of tastes and tunes, a wise choice is to make a bee-line to Beaver Creek for the annual Blues, Brews & Barbecue Festival.

The event, which celebrated its 12th anniversary in 2006, originated as a single-day, mid-May brewfest, but expanded in recent years. By including top-shelf blues, slow-smoked barbecue, and activities for kids, the BB&B has been transformed into a diverse, inclusive and family-friendly affair.

Food booths, picnic tables and a free-to-the-public music stage are set up amidst the boutique shops and restaurants of Beaver Creek Plaza, in and around what serves in winter as an ice skating rink. Nearby, kids splash in a fountain, climb a rock wall, bounce on a bungee trampoline and play mini-golf.

Around noon each festival day, once the morning chill is gone from the pristine Rocky Mountain air, crowds begin to fill the spacious plaza. Senses are piqued as the heady aromas of wood smoke and grilled meats permeate the surroundings and the day's first blues chords emanate from the music stage.

Food always tastes better in the high country, and vendors do a brisk business sating the appetites of ravenous mountain travelers. Barbecue chefs from as far away as Kansas City serve up succulent pulled pork, ribs and other traditional wood-smoked offerings.

Dozens of other food items augments the savory barbecue. Sizzling brats, topped with tangy sauerkraut, are a perennial crowd-pleaser. Some local eateries offer more upscale offerings,

such as Foxnut Restaurant's Crispy Asian Noodle Salad Topped with BBQ Denver Lamb Rib.

The beer tasting is a festival-within-a-festival and takes place just off the plaza in the cushy confines of the five-star Park Hyatt Resort & Spa.

Throughout much of the year, the haute hotel caters to the well-heeled wine-and-cheese crowd. But during the BB&B, affordable beer-tasting/lodging packages entice brew-lovers to the stylish Rocky Mountain retreat for a few days of first-class indulgence.

With exclusively Colorado-made beers, the tasting gives the state's many talented brewers a chance to show off their portfolios of crisp pilsners, deep-flavored stouts and porters and hoppy American ales.

For out-of-state visitors, the tasting is a chance to sample popular Colorado brews such as Breckenridge Brewery's Summerbright, New Belgium's legendary Fat Tire or Dale's Pale Ale, the canned-beer sensation from Oskar Blues.

Devotees of fine fermentables take advantage of the opportunity to sample seasonal and specialty beers—such as Sandlot Brewery's

extraordinary smoked bock—which are normally available only at the breweries.

Many attendees top off the day at the music stage where nationally-acclaimed blues artists keep the dance area hopping with high-energy sets. Recent performers have included guitarist extraordinaire Duke Robillard, soul singer Bettye LaVette and Grammy nominee Charlie Musselwhite, who has been called "the world's greatest living blues harmonica player."

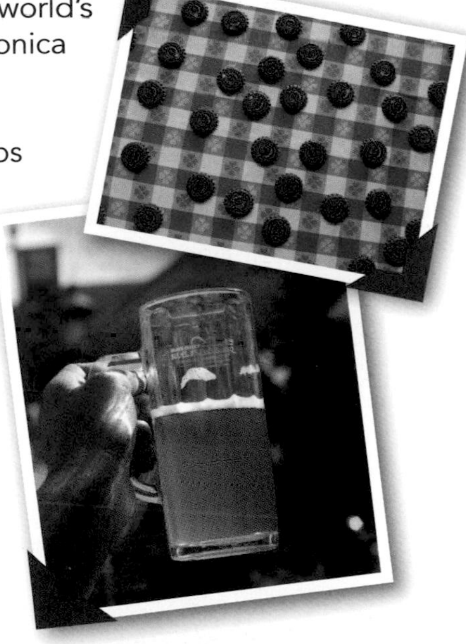

About the time the sun dips below the ridgeline, the festivities end, sending revelers to unwind in hotel rooms and hot tubs. Many, however, will return for the next BB&B. Be-lieve it.

Portions of this review first appeared in The Celebrator Beer News*. Thanks to publisher Tom Dalldorf for permission to excerpt.*

Brew Birds

Craft beer infuses flavor into chicken and poultry, typically bland proteins that need a splash of sauce and color on the grill. Whole chickens can get the flavor of beer without the rude treatment of an aluminum can of beer in the rear. Just use a stainless steel cup full of beer to add moisture as the bird cooks on the grill, and perch the pair on a metal pie plate for stability.

Because boned and skinless poultry tends to look so plain on the plate, pay attention to P.G.M. — pretty grill marks. You can make your boneless, skinless chicken breasts look more appetizing by rotating them on the grill as they cook to leave a perfect cross-hatch of grill grids. The secret? Lightly oil and preheat the grill grid, so the chicken won't stick when you turn it with tongs.

Be sure to remove chicken from the grill as soon as it reaches 2 degrees below food-safe internal temperatures, and let it rest for 5 minutes, covered on a platter, before slicing and serving. As the chicken rests, it will continue to cook and the internal temperature will rise, but the meat will remain juicy and flavorful.

Cilantro Chicken and Black Bean Salad

- 12 ounces fruity amber ale
- ¼ cup olive oil
- ½ cup fresh cilantro leaves
- 2 tablespoons minced garlic
- ½ teaspoon ground cumin
- 1 teaspoon ground coriander
- 1 tablespoon fresh lemon juice
- 1 teaspoon cracked black pepper, or more to taste
- 1 teaspoon kosher salt
- 2 pounds boneless, skinless chicken thighs

Salad:

- 1 can (15 ounces) black beans, drained
- ½ cup chopped celery
- 1 cup chopped cucumber
- ½ cup chopped red bell pepper
- ¼ cup chopped parsley
- ¼ cup minced red onion
- Romaine leaves
- Sliced limes
- Cilantro leaves

1. Place ale, olive oil, cilantro, garlic, cumin, coriander, lemon juice, pepper and salt in blender and purée on HIGH until smooth. Reserve ½ cup mixture for salad and pour remainder into large resealable plastic bag. Add chicken, seal, and chill 8 hours or overnight.

2. Prepare grill. Drain chicken and place on medium-hot grill. Cook 20 to 25 minutes, or until completely cooked through. Chop chicken while still warm and place in bowl with beans. Add celery, cucumber, bell pepper, parsley and onion. Stir well. Taste and adjust seasonings.

3. Serve on a platter of romaine lettuce, with sliced limes and cilantro leaves as garnish.

Makes 4 to 6 servings.

Cilantro Chicken and Black Bean Salad

Grilled Duck with Chipotle Peach Sauce

Chef Scott McGlinchey, owner of the chain of "Q" restaurants in Milwaukee, has supported Wisconsin's craft brewing industry for 2 decades, with beer dinners, tastings, classes, charity benefits, and more. He even created a root beer BBQ sauce for the Sprecher Brewing Co. This recipe showcases his talents in layering flavors in a dish - from the spice rub applied to the duck to the seasonings in the Chipotle Peach Sauce. It's worth the time!

- 2 duck breasts, boned, skin on, about 14 ounces each
- 2 tablespoons paprika
- 1 tablespoon finely ground black pepper
- 1 tablespoon powdered garlic
- 2 tablespoons salt
- 1 tablespoon ground ancho chile
- 1 tablespoon ground cumin
- 1 tablespoon ground coriander
- 1 teapoon ground nutmeg
- 1 teaspoon ground ginger
- 1 teaspoon ground cloves

1. Place duck breasts in large shallow dish. Mix spices and apply to both sides of poultry, pressing into surface. Cover and chill overnight. Prepare peach sauce and chill overnight for best flavor (recipe follows).

2. Prepare grill to medium (350°F) and place duck breasts on grill, skin side down, for 8 to 10 minutes, rotating once during cooking for "p.g.m." (pretty grill marks). Turn and cook another 4 to 5 minutes for rare, 8 minutes for medium-well. Let duck rest 10 minutes before slicing; serve with Chipotle Peach Sauce.

Makes 4 to 6 servings.

Chipotle Peach Sauce

- 1 tablespoon olive oil
- 2 tablespoons chopped shallots
- 2 cups peeled and chopped peaches, pits removed
- 12 ounces summer ale
- 1 teaspoon sauce from chipotle pepper en adobo
- 3 ounces chicken stock

1. Place olive oil and shallots in large skillet, and cook over low heat until shallots are just tender. Add peaches and ale, and simmer until reduced by half, about 30 minutes.

2. Stir in chipotle sauce and chicken stock and simmer 5 minutes. Remove from heat and let cool to lukewarm. Blend in blender on HIGH until smooth, and taste and adjust seasonings.

Makes 1¼ cups.

Grilled Chicken Salad with Porter Tahini Glaze

- 1 pound boneless, skinless chicken breasts
- ⅓ cup tahini (sesame seed paste)
- ½ cup porter
- 1 tablespoon minced garlic
- 1 tablespoon minced fresh rosemary
- 1 tablespoon lemon juice
- Hot pepper sauce to taste
- 1 cup chopped avocado
- 1 tablespoon fresh lime juice
- 1½ tablespoons minced fresh ginger
- ⅓ cup sliced, pitted kalamata or Greek olives
- 1½ cups chopped celery
- 1 cup chopped red or orange bell pepper
- ½ cup chopped snow peas
- ⅓ cup chopped red onion
- Pita pocket bread or romaine lettuce cups

1. Marinate chicken by placing it in large 1-gallon resealable plastic bag and adding tahini, porter, garlic, rosemary, lemon juice and hot pepper sauce, as desired. Seal bag and turn several times to coat chicken pieces evenly. Chill at least 1 hour.

2. Preheat grill to medium-high. Place a sheet of heavy-duty foil on grill; remove chicken from bag and place on top of foil. Cover grill, and cook 7 to 8 minutes. Turn chicken pieces and cook 7 to 8 minutes more, or until chicken reaches internal temperature of 160°F. Remove chicken from grill and cool.

3. In large bowl, mix avocado, lime and ginger, mashing lightly with fork. Add remaining ingredients and stir well to coat lightly with avocado. Chop cooked chicken into bite-size pieces and mix with salad. Serve stuffed in pitas or in romaine lettuce cups.

Makes 4 cups salad.

Dirty Blonde BBQ Chicken Wings

This fiery Dirty Blonde BBQ sauce matches the tangy flavors of tropical fruit with bitter-sweet witbier (chef Ric uses Ommegang Brewery's Witte) and the bright heat of super-hot peppers. Use this as a dipping sauce, slather, glaze or all-purpose fire sauce for friends and enemies alike!

- 1 cup witbier
- 8 ounces honey
- 2 tablespoons diced red onion
- 2 teaspoons ground allspice
- 2 teaspoons ground black pepper
- 2 teaspoons ground turmeric
- ¼ cup orange juice
- ½ cup grapefruit juice
- ½ cup pineapple juice
- ¼ cup diced habañero or scotch bonnet peppers, stemmed and puréed
- 2 ounces cider vinegar
- 2 tablespoons unsalted butter
- 3 lbs fresh chicken wings

1. Place witbier, honey, onion, allspice, pepper, turmeric, juices, peppers, vinegar and butter in a medium saucepan over high heat. Bring to a rolling boil, then turn heat to low, and simmer 20 minutes to reduce by 25 percent.

2. Clean chicken wings of any feathers or excess skin. Brush 1 cup sauce on wings and either grill or bake until crisp, about 15 minutes minutes over medium indirect heat. Do not let sauce flare up. Serve with remaining sauce on the side.

Makes 4 servings.

Spicy Brown Ale Wings

Spicy Brown Ale Brined Wings

The sauce is hotter than one of hockey broadcaster Don Cherry's neck ties, but still toothsome.

- ½ cup brown sugar
- ½ cup kosher salt
- 24 ounces brown ale
- 5 pounds chicken wings, cut into three sections, small tips removed
- 1 cup butter
- 2 tablespoons minced garlic
- ¼ cup minced fresh jalapeños (or mix habañeros and jalapeños)
- ½ cup hot pepper sauce, or more to taste
- ½ cup Sriracha or Asian sweet hot chile sauce
- Pinch ground cinnamon
- 1 teaspoon finely ground black pepper
- 24 bamboo skewers, at least 10 inches long, soaked in water
- 2 tablespoons black or toasted sesame seeds for garnish (optional)

1. Mix brown sugar, salt and brown ale in large gallon bowl and whisk until dissolved to make a brine. Place wings in bowl and stir to coat. Cover and chill 4 to 8 hours.

2. Melt butter in large skillet and add garlic and jalapeños. Sauté over low heat until jalapeños are tender. Add hot pepper sauce, Sriracha, cinnamon and pepper. Mix well and simmer 3 minutes. Place in blender and purée until smooth.

3. Prepare grill. Drain wings from brine and thread on skewers, 3 to 4 pieces per skewer. Keep pieces of similar sizes together so chicken will cook evenly. Place skewers on grill over indirect heat (or use a grill basket). Cook 25 minutes or until very brown and crispy, turning every 5 minutes. Arrange cooked wings on platter, spoon prepared chile sauce over evenly, and sprinkle with black sesame seeds.

Makes 6 servings.

Hops and Herbs Chopped Chicken Sandwiches

- 12 ounces American IPA or hoppy pale ale
- 2 tablespoons olive oil
- 1 teaspoon lemon juice
- 2 tablespoons fresh marjoram
- 2 tablespoons fresh basil
- 1 tablespoon fresh oregano
- ¼ cup minced green onion
- ½ teaspoon cayenne
- ½ teaspoon grated horseradish, or more to taste
- 3 pounds trimmed boneless, skinless chicken thighs

1. Place ale, olive oil, lemon juice, marjoram, basil, oregano, onion, cayenne and horseradish in blender; blend on HIGH until smooth. Reserve ½ cup mixture; pour remainder into large glass dish. Add chicken thighs, stir to coat, and cover with plastic wrap. Chill at least 4 hours.

2. Prepare grill; drain chicken and cook until done, about 20 minutes. Remove from grill and let rest 5 minutes. Chop well and mix with remaining ale-herb mixture. Serve on sliced rolls with desired garnish.

Makes 4 to 6 servings.

Raspberry Ale Grilled Duck

¼ cup olive oil
¼ cup minced shallots
1 tablespoon minced garlic
½ cup fruit-only apricot or blackberry spread
12 ounces raspberry ale or framboise lambic
1 teaspoon ground ginger
½ teaspoon ground cayenne
1 teaspoon turmeric
Pinch allspice
Pinch ground cardamom
1 teaspoon kosher salt
1 teaspoon freshly ground black pepper
6 duck breasts, about 4 to 5 ounces each, scored
Salad of baby spinach greens, chopped toasted pecans, and fresh raspberries or blackberries

1. Place olive oil in small skillet over low heat and add shallots, garlic and your choice of fruit spread. Simmer and stir 3 minutes. Scrape mixture into blender and add ale, remaining spices and seasonings. Cover and blend on HIGH until smooth. Reserve ¼ cup mixture to toss with salad, and pour remainder in large resealable plastic bag. Add duck to bag, seal and chill overnight.

2. Prepare grill. Drain duck and cook over indirect heat until duck is medium-rare. Turn several times to get grill marks, and cook a total of 20 to 30 minutes, depending on thickness of duck. Do not overcook. Let duck rest, covered on a platter, for 5 minutes. Slice thinly and serve with salad and desired garnish.

Makes 6 servings.

Cajun Beer Can Chicken

Several craft brewers now can their beer, from the 21st Amendment in San Francisco, CA to Capital Brewery in Madison, Wisconsin. Or, if you choose you use a bottled beer, use a chicken-on-a-throne roaster made of stainless steel to hold whatever style of beer you enjoy. Steven Raichlen of BBQ-U, the grilling maven, sells a BBQ accessory for just this purpose. Thanks to Terri Pischoff Wuerthner, CCP, author of IN A CAJUN KITCHEN, St. Martin's Press (2006) for sharing this recipe.

Terri says, "This is usually cooked on a barbecue in Cajun Country, but it also works well on a baking sheet in the oven (at 350°F for 1 to 1½ hours). It is probably the easiest-to-prepare method of roasting a chicken, and results in a moist, flavorful bird with a dark, crisp, crust."

1 roasting chicken, about 4 pounds
1 tablespoon olive oil
3 tablespoons Cajun Spice Mix (available in spice section of markets), divided
1 12-ounce can beer

1. Set up grill, whether charcoal or gas, with heat on one side so chicken will not be over direct heat. Preheat barbecue before placing chicken on grill. Rub chicken on all sides with oil, then sprinkle skin evenly with 2 tablespoons spice mix.

2. Pour about ⅓ of beer into a glass and enjoy it while you cook chicken. Make two or three additional holes in top of beer can with a church-key can opener. Add remaining one tablespoon spice mix to can (beer may foam when you add spice mix).

3. Gently place chicken cavity onto beer can on a flat work surface, and spread out legs, moving them about until two legs in front and beer can in back form a stable balance. Tuck wing tips behind chicken's back.

4. Place chicken on preheated grill, over indirect heat. Cook, covered, until juices run clear when thigh is pierced with a knife, and internal temperature reaches 175°F. This will take from 1 to 1½ hours, depending on size of chicken (check after 1 hour.) Use tongs to remove chicken from barbecue and let rest for 10 minutes before carving. Use caution to avoid spilling hot beer.

Makes 4 to 6 servings.

Note: perch the chicken, can end down, on a cheap aluminum pie pan to catch drips and make a stable base on the grill. —L.S.

San Andreas Malts Oyster BBQ

Hot Oysters and Fresh Beer for Homebrew Cooks

by Jay Brooks
www.brookston.org

Every year since 1978, the members of the San Andreas Malts, a San Francisco homebrew club, have been throwing themselves a party. What began in club founder Terry Brandborg's back yard has evolved into the club's biggest event of the year. And while many homebrew clubs have get-togethers, this is the only one we know of that celebrates with both hand-crafted beer and barbecued oysters.

The picnic is now held in a state park in Pacifica, a quaint coastal town along Highway One a few miles south of San Francisco. The lush green space is ideal, with picnic tables and a bank of grills. In late April, when the event is held, everywhere you look is green, from the wide-open grassy plain to the surrounding thickly wooded hills.

The club supplies all the oysters, and members and their families each bring a potluck dish to share. And most importantly, there are more than a dozen kegs of varying sizes. Some are filled with homebrewed beer while others are commercial beers donated by Emeritus members such as Alec Moss of Half Moon Bay Brewing and Grant Johnston of Black Diamond Brewing.

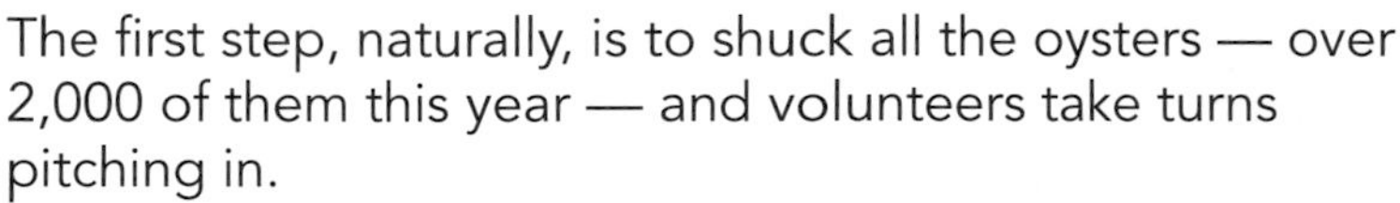

The first step, naturally, is to shuck all the oysters — over 2,000 of them this year — and volunteers take turns pitching in.

Some are grilled plain, but the majority are grilled with one of two sauces developed specifically for the barbecue. The first, a traditional red sauce created by Mark Kornmann, is created on the fly without measuring any of the ingredients. He mixes ketchup, horseradish, lemon juice, and dried cayenne peppers to taste. He then fills an empty ketchup bottle with his sauce and as the oysters are grilling, gives each a squirt. Mark, pictured here, says the taste would be better if the grills were covered. "That way the oysters would have a more intense smoked flavor."

The other sauce is a bit more unusual. It's a pesto-based sauce created by Chuck Cihak. Chuck has refined his recipe over many years and is justly proud of it.

He starts with generous handfuls of walnuts and pine nuts, to which he adds a half stick butter, 3 cloves garlic, 5 peppercorns, a tablespoon coarse salt, a tablespoon lemon juice, 3 cups packed basil leaves, 4 oz. grated Romano cheese and 4 oz. grated Parmesan cheese. Then he runs it through a Cuisinart, slowly pouring in 1½ cups olive oil. Chuck, shown here with some of his oysters, then hand ladles his pesto sauce onto each oyster before grilling.

Oysters and beer have had a long and illustrious relationship. The sharp, briny flavors of the oyster have long been known to pair beautifully with stouts and porters. It most likely began when the porter style was very popular and oysters were quite plentiful, which made them cheap, as well. Later, stouts like Guinness were often paired with oysters and some were even named oyster stouts like Marston's Oyster Stout. But it wasn't until modern times that actual oysters were put into the beer itself. Several now include oysters themselves in the brewing process such as Ventnor Brewery and Bushy's, both in England. Here in the U.S., several craft brewers put real shellfish into their oyster stouts, including Dogfish Head Brewing, Rogue Ales, Southampton Publick House and 21st Amendment.

Other beer styles that pair nicely with oysters are helles, gueuze, IPAs, pilsners, and strong Belgian ales, like dubbels and triples.

"For many years this has been the most popular event that the club hosts," says San Andreas Malts president Dave Suurballe, pictured here with his wife Honoria. "Usually at monthly meetings we'll have maybe a dozen people. But hundreds will attend the Oyster BBQ."

In fact the picnic grounds were full most of the day, with homebrewers and their families enjoying the warm sunshine with beer, food and oysters.

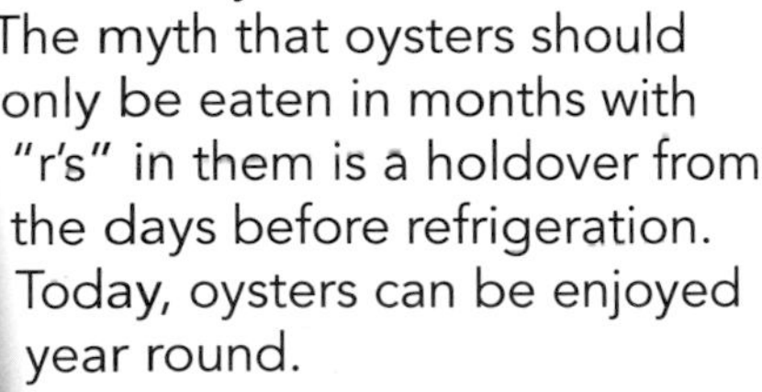

The myth that oysters should only be eaten in months with "r's" in them is a holdover from the days before refrigeration. Today, oysters can be enjoyed year round.

As these picnic-goers already know, oysters are not only delicious but are also very nutritious with plenty of protein, carbohydrates and lipids. They also include numerous vitamins such as A, B, C and D plus calcium, copper, iodine, iron, magnesium, manganese, phosphorus and zinc.

All this for a measly 75 calories, though that's without the BBQ sauce.

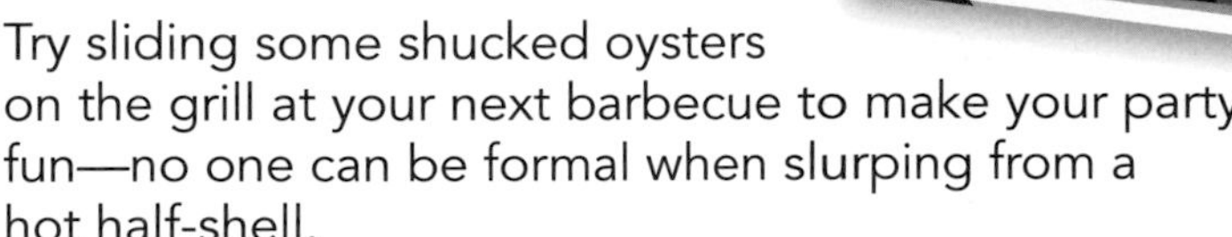

Try sliding some shucked oysters on the grill at your next barbecue to make your party fun—no one can be formal when slurping from a hot half-shell.

Text and photography courtesy of Jay Brooks, www.brookston.org

Seared Seafood

ALL ABOUT BEER publisher Dan Bradford and I often debate beer pairings. He believes that shellfish should always be paired with dark ale, especially stouts. One of the most famous food festivals in the Pacific Northwest is the Oyster Festival at The Brooklyn Seafood House of Seattle, Washington, where the Kumamato oysters are served in ale shooters. But come summertime and the grilling season, I shy away from the heavier, darker brews. Despite the classic match, I prefer to sip a gently spicy witbier, or best of all, a robust American pale ale, with seafood.

Several tools make seafood simpler to cook; a grill grate or mesh grid to hold shrimp, a fish grill basket, and wood planks.

Cooking fish on the grill is so easy with wood planks. Just soak the wood plank (typically untreated cedar or alderwood) for an hour in water. Prepare the fish and place it on the bare, damp wood. Put the plank on the grill and cover. The wood will char and add smoky aromas while keeping the fish moist and tender. And clean-up consists of crumpling the plank into the charcoal fire, or if cooking over propane, removing the plank and letting the wood cool before tossing it into the compost heap.

Grilled Seafood Stew

In this recipe, all the vegetables are cut into thick round slices, seared on the grill grate for smoky flavor, and tossed into a stew pot on a side burner or in the central hot spot over the coals. The hot Italian sausage makes the broth rich and spicy.

- 1 large Spanish onion, peeled and sliced
- 1 large potato, peeled and sliced
- 6 ounces spicy Italian sausage
- 1 green bell pepper, sliced
- 1 minced fresh jalapeño
- 12 ounces brown ale
- 1 cup water
- 1 tablespoon Old Bay seasoning mix
- 12 clams
- 12 large green-lipped New Zealand mussels, cleaned
- 12 large sea scallops
- 12 large shrimp
- Salt and pepper to taste
- 6 wedges lemon

1. Prepare grill to medium heat. Brush sliced onion, potato and pepper with oil and sear on both sides. Place sausages on grill. Place onion, potato, pepper, ale, water and Old Bay seasoning mix into cast iron Dutch oven or flame-safe deep pan over grill or side burner. Simmer until potato is completely tender.

2. While vegetables simmer, continue to grill sausages until completely cooked. Remove from grill to cutting board with grooves to collect juices. When cool enough to handle, slice sausages. Add sliced cooked sausage and reserved juices to Dutch oven with vegetable mixture.

3. Place clams and mussels in Dutch oven or deep pan. Sear scallops and shrimp on both sides on grill grid, and add to Dutch oven. Cook just until shellfish open and

remove from heat. Season with salt and pepper. Serve in large shallow bowls with sausage and vegetable stew, lemon wedges and grilled garlic bread.

Makes 4 to 6 servings.

Bacon-Wrapped Grilled Shrimp

- 24 jumbo shrimp, deveined and shelled, tails left on
- 12 ounces stout
- 12 thin slices bacon or pancetta
- ¼ cup Dijon mustard
- 2 tablespoons minced chives or green onion leaves
- Wooden toothpicks

1. Place shrimp and 8 ounces stout in large resealable plastic bag. Seal, turn several times to coat shrimp, and chill. Marinate overnight.
2. Cook bacon in large skillet over low heat 2 to 3 minutes, until pliable and fat is barely translucent. Do not let brown. Remove and drain on paper towel. When cool enough to handle, cut bacon in half to make 24 short strips, about 3 inches long. Mix mustard and chives, and brush on one side of each bacon strip. Wrap bacon around shrimp, using a toothpick to secure meat in place.
3. Prepare grill to medium heat. Place shrimp on grill grid or in grill basket. Baste often with reserved 4 ounces stout. Cook until bacon is browned evenly and shrimp is cooked through, about 5 minutes. Serve immediately.

Makes 12 servings.

Porter Ginger Salmon Skewers

- 12 ounces porter
- 1 tablespoon minced ginger
- 2 tablespoons minced garlic
- 1 teaspoon ground white pepper
- 1 tablespoon soy sauce
- 1½ pound salmon, skin and bones removed, cut into 1-inch cubes
- 1 medium sweet onion, peeled
- 1 large red bell pepper
- 14 large mushrooms
- 8 bamboo skewers, 10 or 12 inches long, or thin metal skewers

1. Mix porter, ginger, garlic, pepper and soy sauce in bowl. Reserve ⅓ cup for basting. Pour remaining marinade into resealable plastic bag. Add cubed salmon, seal, and turn several times to coat well. Chill at least 1 hour.
2. Soak skewers in water. Prepare vegetables by washing and slicing into bite-sized chunks or thick slices, as desired.
3. Thread alternating pieces of vegetables and salmon on skewers. Prepare grill. Cook skewers over medium heat, basting often with reserved ⅓ cup marinade. Skewers are ready when salmon is orange and flaky and vegetables are tender. Serve with rice or salad.

Makes 4 to 6 servings.

Porter Ginger
Salmon Skewers

Grilled Pilsner Pepper Crab

Grill the crabs over indirect heat (over a double thickness of foil) to keep the meat from drying out.

- 2 fresh cleaned crabs (2 to 3 pounds each)
- 2 cups Pilsner Pepper Sauce (recipe follows)
- 3 tablespoons olive oil, plus more for oiling grill
- 3 tablespoons butter
- ¼ cup slivered garlic
- 2 tablespoons fresh lime juice

1. Bring large pot of salted water to a boil, drop in crabs, and cook exactly 3 minutes per pound. Remove immediately and plunge into bowl filled with 2 bottles ice cold pilsner and 2 cups ice to stop cooking. (This step may be done a few hours ahead.)

2. Crack crabs at joints so they absorb marinade. Place crabs in a large shallow pan, cover with pilsner pepper sauce, cover with plastic wrap, and chill at least 1 to 4 hours. Light grill and let burn down to a medium fire. Drain crabs, oil grill well, and cook crabs over indirect medium heat, tented with foil, until cooked through, about 8 minutes.

3. Heat olive oil and butter in small saucepan over medium-low heat. Add garlic and cook and stir until garlic turns golden, about 2 minutes. Add lime juice and remove from heat. Serve crabs with melted butter if desired.

Makes 4 servings.

Pilsner Pepper Sauce

- 8 ounces pilsner
- Juice of one lime
- Freshly ground black pepper, to taste
- ¼ cup minced garlic
- ¼ cup Dijon mustard
- 1 cup olive oil

1. Mix all ingredients in a blender on HIGH until smooth. Use as a marinade for seafood or chicken.

Makes 2¼ cups.

Grilled Pear & Salmon Patties with PNW Pale Ale

- 1½ pounds fresh boneless, skinless salmon fillets
- ⅓ cup peeled and grated pear
- ¼ cup pale ale (Pacific Northwest or hoppy ale)
- ½ cup toasted panko bread crumbs (see p. 180)
- 1 egg white
- 1½ tablespoons chopped chives
- 1 teaspoon grated ginger
- 1 tablespoon hoisin sauce
- Freshly ground black pepper, to taste

1. Pulse salmon in food processor until coursely ground. Mix with remaining ingredients. Chill 8 hours.
2. Form 6 patties (¼ pound each) and cook on oiled sheet of heavy duty foil over low heat on grill. Add wood chips and cover grill to get extra smoky flavor. Cook 8 minutes, or until firm and cooked through. Serve with wasabi mayonnaise and sliced cucumber.

Makes 6 servings.

Malt Monster Shrimp

Use a bock lager or immensely malty dark ale to make these shrimp. They will turn a luscious dark gold color, thanks to the malt caramelization on the grill.

- 12 ounces bock lager
- ½ cup fresh-squeezed orange juice
- 1 tablespoon chopped fresh flat-leaf parsley
- 1 tablespoon minced garlic
- 2 tablespoons hot pepper sauce
- 2 tablespoons toasted sesame chili oil
- 1 teaspoon salt
- 2 pounds large shrimp, shelled and cleaned (total 30 pieces)
- 10 skewers

1. Mix bock, juice, parsley, garlic, pepper sauce, chili oil and salt in a large resealable plastic bag. Add shrimp and seal. Chill overnight.

2. Prepare grill. Remove shrimp from bag and drain marinade. Thread onto metal skewers or soaked bamboo skewers, 3 per skewer. Grill shrimp on a grate or a grilling basket over medium heat, about 2 minutes each side. Serve immediately.

Makes 10 servings.

Hoisin-Porter Halibut

- ¼ cup hoisin sauce
- ¼ cup porter
- 2 tablespoons minced green onion
- 2 pounds halibut fillet
- Mixed salad: arugula, spinach, grated carrot, chopped celery, sliced tomatoes

1. Mix hoisin, porter and green onion. Prepare grill to medium-low. Brush porter mixture over halibut, and grill over indirect heat for 10 to 15 minutes, depending on thickness of fillet.
2. Prepare salad and arrange on platter. Top with cooked halibut and serve.

Makes 4 servings.

Two-Hearted Grilled Gravlax

Chef Eric Gillish uses Bell's Two-Hearted Ale, winner of the first Alpha King Challenge, as the base for gravlax.

- 1 large salmon filet (approx. 4 pounds, skin on)
- 1 cup chopped fresh dill leaves (remove stems)
- 1 pound kosher salt
- 1 pound brown sugar
- 24 ounces hoppy amber ale
- 2 English cucumbers

1. Lay two 22-inch-long pieces of heavy-duty extra-wide foil side-by-side on counter. Bring together edges in center, crimping one-inch to make a 30x22-inch sheet. Place foil on half-sheet pan with raised edges. Cover foil completely with plastic wrap, and lay salmon, skin side down, on the plastic.
2. Cover salmon with fresh dill leaves. Dust with 1 cup each of kosher salt and sugar. Pour 2½ cups ale over salmon. Fold plastic wrap so that fish is submerged in ale. Crimp foil edges upward and together to wrap well. Chill overnight or 24 hours.
3. Remove salmon from foil and plastic wraps. Place on wire rack fitted inside a half-sheet pan so fish can drain as it cures. Cover fish with remaining salt and sugar. Wrap pan completely in plastic wrap and chill 2 days to cure the salmon.
4. Remove salmon from wrap and brush off excess salt and sugar. Pour remaining cup of ale over salmon to rinse off excess. Keep salmon chilled until ready to cook. Prepare grill. Sear salmon, skin side down, before serving. Cut into thin slices and serve on thick slices of English cucumber.

Makes about 24 servings.

Lemon Weiss Grilled Red Snapper

- 4 stalks lemongrass
- Juice of one lemon
- 12 ounces weiss beer
- 1 gutted red snapper, about 3 pounds
- 1 teaspoon lemon pepper
- 1 teaspoon sea salt
- 2 tablespoons canola oil
- Garnish: Sliced lemon and cucumber

1. Bruise lemongrass stalks with blunt edge of a knife, but do not chop. Place in large dish with lemon juice and weiss beer; add snapper. Cover and chill 1 hour. Turn fish and chill again at least 1 hour.

2. Prepare grill to medium. Brush grill grate with oil. Place lemongrass stalks on grill, positioned away from open flame for indirect cooking, and place fish on top of lemongrass. Sprinkle fish with lemon pepper and sea salt. Cover and cook 15 minutes. Use large spatula to turn fish and cook 15 minutes more. Fish should flake easily away from bone. Use spatula to lift whole fish to serving platter. Garnish with slices of lemon and cucumber.

Makes 4 to 6 servings.

Blues, Brews & BBQs at Mount Maunganui, New Zealand

A recent odyssey to New Zealand in search of brews and BBQ could be called "Epic."

Maybe that's because it's the name of one of several new ales launched at the largest fest devoted to beer & BBQ on the North Island, the Mt. Maunganui Brews, Blues & BBQs festival.

Epic is a hoppy ale made by the Steam Brewing Co. of Auckland in homage to classic California pale ales. "Epic Pale Ale is massively dry hopped with US Cascade hops, which most US craft beer drinkers could appreciate but quite foreign to New Zealand drinkers," says the brewer

Luke Nicholas (also publisher of the NZ Real Beer Pages), pictured at right at the fest.

"New Zealanders are accustomed to very light lagers, so we are taking a risk in launching an ale that's got a lot of hops bitterness and big malt flavor," says Nicholas. "We plan on doing lots of tastings and attending festivals to help educate beer drinkers."

To help spur taste-testing at the Mt. Maunganui fest, the pub served a peppery jerk chicken sandwich, shown prepared by Epic brewer Nigel Shaw at the flattop grill. The infamous jerk chicken sandwich was spiced just enough to increase thirst, a strategy that kept the tent packed.

About 12,000 people enjoyed sunshine, beer, barbecue and the blues at the festival. The Mt. Maunganui Brews, Blues & BBQs fest draws about two dozen breweries and at least a dozen grill chefs from area restaurants and caterers. Entire families come and pitch tents at the park, to feast and listen to music. The atmosphere is boisterous under the beer tents, yet friendly

and relaxed when basking under the hot summer sun. Blues performers take the stage, with acts running every hour from noon to night.

Organizer David Mustard has worked with Tauranga Table for 11 years to put on the event at Blake Park in the shadow of Mt. Maunganui. He believes that beer and barbecue make "a superb match." The Brews, Blues & BBQs festival is held at other 2 other venues in addition to Blake Park, but the backdrop of Mt. Maunganui is the most scenic. All the fest tickets sell out in mere hours, so visitors need to find entry tickets for sale through TradeMe.co.nz, the Kiwi online auction site.

Vendors offer plenty of choices. Don't expect to find Memphis or Kansas City style hot red sauce over smoked pork - it's not the American version of barbecue. Barbecued chicken with coconut lime sauce, Thai-spiced fish burgers with onion jam, Lone Star ribs, and massive beef roasts rubbed with pepper all cooked on grills at the park, with aromas tempting fest-goers. There were also tender New Zealand lamb

shanks roasted and drenched in Asian sweet chili sauce.

I sampled everything from a boysenberry-flavored homebrew, to an organic ale made by the White Cliffs Brewery of Taranaki, to the new Epic. It was also a treat to taste a crisp pale ale from Crouchers Brewing Co., tapped at its first booth at the fest. Dark lagers are very popular in NZ, especially the Mac's Black, made in Wellington.

However, some of the country's best small brewers were not there - Emerson, Founders, Limburg, and Tuatara passed up the fest, while more mainstream brands such as Tui and Speight's had large tents. To get a true taste of the full range of NZ craft beer, you'll need to travel farther afield than the shadow of Mt. Maunganui on a single afternoon. But this fest is a good start! —L.S.

WWW.BLUESBREWS.CO.NZ

Sides & Salads

I love to grill all year 'round, especially in summer. When local farmers markets have loads of abundant greens and vegetables, it's easy to make a meal from grilled salads, flatbreads and side dishes.

Salmon, chicken, shrimp or grilled veggies on top of baby spinach or arugula tastes delicious. Corn, peppers, zucchini, onions, sweet potatoes, squash and eggplant can all be grilled, chopped and tossed into the salad bowl.

You can grill croutons for a garlicky Caesar salad or panzanella, an Italian salad made of bread with chopped tomatoes and fixings. Just add a few large cubes of sourdough bread or herbed hazelnut flatbread (p. 162). Thread onto skewers of veggies, grill with a brushing of olive oil mixed with minced garlic, place skewers atop bowls of chopped romaine salad, and dust lightly with grated Parmesan cheese. The cheese melts on top of the warm veggies and tastes wonderful served with a hoppy IPA.

Even veggies that are notoriously awful with wine, such as asparagus or eggplant, taste divine with craft beer.
The following will inspire grill cooks, with plenty of craft beer flavors to enhance the results.

Sweet and Sour IPA Slaw

- 1 cup dates, pitted and chopped
- 1 cup peeled and shredded carrots
- 1 cup shredded green cabbage
- 1 cup broccoli slaw (shredded stalks)
- ⅓ cup India Pale Ale
- ⅓ cup sweetened coconut milk
- 1 teaspoon tamarind paste or lemon juice concentrate
- Pinch salt
- ½ teaspoon ground cayenne or other chile, or to taste

1. Toss dates, carrots, cabbage and broccoli slaw in a medium bowl.

2. Place IPA, coconut milk, tamarind paste, salt and cayenne in small saucepan over low heat. Cook and stir until warm and tamarind paste (if using) is emulsified. Taste and adjust seasonings. Remove from heat and pour hot dressing over slaw, tossing well to coat evenly. Chill at least 1 hour before serving.

Makes 6 to 8 servings (½ cup portion).

Sweet and Sour IPA Slaw

Party Beer Salsa

This recipe comes from beerbistro, and makes enough to serve a crowd.

- 3 tablespoons olive oil
- ¼ cup Spanish onion, peeled and diced
- 3 garlic cloves, peeled and minced
- ¼ cup serrano pepper, finely diced (protect hands and eyes when handling hot peppers)
- ¼ cup green pepper, finely diced
- ¼ cup tomato paste
- 14 to 16 plum tomatoes, seeded, finely diced, drained
- 1½ cups Vienna lager
- ½ teaspoon ground cumin
- ¾ cup cooked black beans
- ¾ cup corn kernels, fresh cut from grilled whole cob
- ¼ cup coriander, fresh, chopped
- ¼ cup fresh basil, chopped
- Juice of 2 limes
- Sugar (optional)

1. Place olive oil, onions, garlic and peppers in stainless steel pot over medium-high heat. Cook and stir until onions are softened but not browned.
2. Add tomato paste, then cook and stir for 5 minutes. Add plum tomatoes, lager and cumin to pot. Bring to a boil, then lower heat and let simmer until thickened to desired thickness.
3. Stir in black beans and corn, bring back to a simmer, and remove from heat. Add coriander, basil and lime juice to taste. If very acidic, add 1 teaspoon sugar.
4. Let cool and pack in glass or stainless steel container; seal. Refrigerate. Can be refrigerated up to 3 to 4 days.

Makes 8 cups.

Barley Wine Grilled Potatoes

3 cups chopped new potatoes
2 ounces barley wine
1 ounce olive oil
1 ounce aged Balsamic or sherry vinegar
2 to 4 cloves garlic, chopped
1 teaspoon dried rosemary or thyme
1 to 3 teaspoons honey if barley wine is bitter
Salt and freshly cracked pepper to taste

1. Mix all ingredients and marinate 2 hours. Drain and reserve marinade. Place potatoes in grill basket and grill over a medium charcoal fire, turning when browned. Baste with reserved barley wine marinade. When tender, stir potatoes back into pan with any remaining marinade and toss. Serve hot.

Makes 4 servings.

Pike Pub Mustard

Enjoy this easy recipe from Gary Marx, executive chef at the family-owned Pike Brewing Company in Seattle's historic Pike Place Public Market. The chef uses Pike XXXXX Stout and craft barley malt vinegar brewed by Spinnakers Gastro Brew Pub in Victoria, B.C., Canada.

1 cup whole-grain coarse mustard
½ cup oatmeal stout
¼ cup dark brown sugar
1 teaspoon cider or malt vinegar
2 tablespoons unhopped barley malt extract

1. Blend all ingredients. Keeps covered in refrigerator for up to 1 month. Makes 1½ cups.

Grilled Herbed Hazelnut Flatbread

A good brown ale will make the dough both flavorful and slightly sticky, so be sure to oil your hands before forming the flatbread. Flour also absorbs water from the air, so add the flour to the beer until the dough forms a sticky ball while kneading. Grill on a preheated baking stone for even browning.

- 1 cup chopped hazelnuts
- 12 ounces brown ale
- 2 tablespoons brown sugar
- 2½ teaspoons rapid-rising dry yeast (1 envelope)
- 1½ to 2 cups white enriched bread flour
- 1½ cups whole wheat pastry flour
- 1 teaspoon salt
- ¼ cup softened unsalted butter
- 2 to 3 tablespoons heavy cream, if needed
- ¼ cup hazelnut oil or olive oil, for greasing bowl and dough
- ¼ cup semolina or corn grits, divided
- 2 tablespoons fresh sage
- 1 to 2 tablespoons coarse kosher or sea salt
- Baking stone soaked in water

1. Toast hazelnuts in large skillet over medium heat, stirring constantly. When nuts turn golden, pour in brown ale and sugar, and simmer until sugar dissolves. Remove from heat and let cool to 104°F.

2. When cooled, strain 1 cup ale from skillet and check temperature to make sure it is still at 104°F. Stir in yeast.

3. While yeast dissolves, sift together bread flour and whole wheat pastry flour into mixing bowl. Place ale-yeast mixture in bowl of electric mixer fitted with bread hook. Add nuts and remaining ale from skillet to bowl, and add 2 cups

flour. Mix on low for 1 minute, add salt, and add butter by the tablespoonful. Add enough of remaining flour to form a sticky ball of dough, shaking flour slowly from 1-cup measure into mixer. Stop mixer and scrape down sides of bowl several times. Don't add too much flour all at once. If you do and dough seems crumbly, add heavy cream, 1 tablespoon at a time, stopping mixer and scraping down sides of bowl after each addition. Dough should be soft and springy after 8 to 10 minutes of kneading.

4. Oil large bowl with 2 tablespoons hazelnut oil, and place dough in bowl, turning to grease it on all sides. Cover with damp cloth and set in a warm spot to rise until doubled in size. Oil your hands and punch dough flat.

5. Place dough on well-soaked baking stone sprayed with cooking oil and sprinkled with semolina. Roll or press dough

(Recipe continued on page 164)

(Recipe continued from page163)

with your hands and flatten to match size of baking stone. Dough may be rectangular or round but should be about 1-inch thick throughout.

6. Oil surface of the flatbread liberally. Prick dough with a fork all over. Chop sage and kosher salt together, and sprinkle over formed flatbread.

7. Place baking stone on grill and start fire or ignite grill. Do not put cold baking stone on hot grill, as it may crack. Loosely tent baking stone with foil. Close grill cover. Cook 20 minutes or until golden. Remove from grill and let cool 15 minutes before slicing. Dough will continue to cook on stone after removing from grill, so do not overbake.

Makes 8 servings.

Grilled Herbed
Hazelnut Flatbread

Brined Grilled Eggplant

Bill Brand of the Oakland Tribune rhapsodized about this recipe when he tried it at the grilling with beer tasting held at the Cathedral Hill Hotel. It was prepared with Russian River's Damnation, and tasted heavenly.

- 2 eggplants, each weighing about 1 pound, washed, peeled, trimmed, and cut into thin or medium-thick slices
- 24 ounces tripel
- 2 tablespoons kosher salt
- 2 tablespoons chopped parsley
- ¼ cup chopped basil
- 2 tablespoons chopped mint
- 2 tablespoons chopped marjoram
- 2 tablespoons chopped garlic
- ¼ cup olive oil
- ¼ cup pine nuts
- ¼ cup macadamia nuts

1. Place eggplant slices in extra-large resealable plastic bag and add tripel and salt. Seal and turn, letting eggplant brine for at least 1 hour. Or, place eggplant slices in shallow glass dish, add brine and cover with plastic wrap; chill. Unwrap and turn eggplant over twice to brine evenly.
2. In food processor fitted with metal chopping blade, chop herbs, garlic, olive oil and nuts until a paste forms.
3. Remove eggplant from brine, and drain well. Smear herb paste on one side of eggplant slices. Grill over indirect heat until eggplant is tender, about 5 to 10 minutes depending on thickness. Do not let nut mixture burn.

Makes 4 to 6 servings.

Brewer's Mustard Coleslaw

- ¼ cup canola oil
- 1 teaspoon celery seeds
- 1 teaspoon brown mustard seeds
- 1 tablespoon brown sugar
- 1 teaspoon red pepper flakes
- ¼ cup prepared beer mustard
- ½ cup amber ale
- 2 teaspoons malt vinegar
- 1 cup finely shredded collards
- ¼ cup dried currants
- 4 cups finely shredded red and green cabbage
- 1 cup shredded carrots
- 1 cup minced green scallions
- ¼ cup dry roasted peanuts, chopped

1. Place canola oil in a medium skillet and add celery and mustard seeds. Heat over low heat until mustard seeds start to pop, then stir in brown sugar, red pepper flakes, mustard, ale and vinegar. Stir in finely shredded collard greens and simmer 5 minutes. Add currants and stir. Remove from heat.
2. Mix cabbage, carrots, scallions and peanuts. Toss with warm greens and dressing to coat evenly. Set aside to chill.

Makes 4 to 6 servings.

Rauchbier BBQ Beans

No barbecue would be complete without some kind of bean dish to serve on the side. These are tangy, sweet, and completely tender.

- ½ cup diced Canadian bacon
- 1 cup minced onion
- 1 cup rauchbier or smoked ale
- 2 28-ounce cans baked beans
- 1 cup barley malt extract
- ¼ cup molasses
- ¼ cup prepared brown mustard
- 1 cup tomato chili sauce
- 1 tablespoon Worcestershire sauce
- Several dashes hot pepper sauce, to taste

1. Cook Canadian bacon and onion in large cast iron saucepan or Dutch oven over low heat for 2 minutes. Add rauchbier or smoked ale.

2. Drain fat from baked beans and add to saucepan along with remaining ingredients. Stir to mix. Cook on grill or side burner for 1 hour over low heat. Stir often.

Makes 8 servings.

Note: The flavor of the beans improves with time, so you may make them 1 day ahead and reheat.

Grilled Potato Salad

Dressing:

- ⅓ cup canola oil
- ⅓ cup amber ale
- 3 ounces light cream cheese
- 1 teaspoon caraway seeds
- ½ teaspoon celery seeds
- 1 teaspoon brown mustard seeds
- 1 teaspoon kosher salt
- ¼ teaspoon red pepper flakes
- 2 tablespoons minced parsley

1. Place all ingredients in blender, and blend on HIGH until smooth.
2. Chill at least 1 hour to meld flavors.

Salad:

- 2 tablespoons olive oil
- 2 pounds small red potatoes
- 1 cup chopped celery (2 stalks)
- ½ cup English cucumber, peeled and sliced
- 3 scallions, minced (include some green leaves)
- ⅓ cup dill pickle relish
- ⅓ cup chopped daikon radish
- Salt and pepper to taste

1. Toss potatoes with olive oil and grill over indirect heat until tender; turn often and do not let burn. Remove from heat and when cool enough to handle, chop into bite-size pieces.
2. Mix chopped potatoes and remaining vegetables in large bowl and mix well with dressing. Add salt and black pepper, if desired.

Makes 6 to 8 servings.

Grilled Corn & Rice Salad

Grilled Corn & Rice Salad

Mass-produced lager beer is often brewed with corn and rice "adjuncts." But this salad tastes anything but mass-market!

- ¼ cup pilsner or German Helles lager
- 1 tablespoon melted butter
- ½ teaspoon salt
- ½ teaspoon ground black pepper
- ½ teaspoon ground chile powder
- 3 ears fresh sweet corn, shucked
- ½ cup red bell pepper, seeded and diced
- ¼ cup minced cilantro
- ¼ cup chopped green onion
- 1 large ripe tomato, seeded and diced (about ¾ cup)
- 2 cups cooked white rice

Dressing:

- 1 tablespoon lime juice
- 2 tablespoons lager
- ¼ teaspoon cayenne pepper, or more to taste
- 1 tablespoon olive oil

1. Mix ¼ cup lager, melted butter, salt, pepper and chile powder. Brush ears of corn with beer mixture and grill over medium heat for 10 to 20 minutes, or until tender. Set aside to cool.

2. Mix bell pepper, cilantro, onion, tomato and rice in large, shallow serving dish. Cut kernels away from corn cobs, and stir into salad, along with any reserved juices. Mix lime juice, 2 tablespoons lager, cayenne and olive oil in a small bowl. Pour over salad and toss well.

Makes 6 servings.

Cook-off at the Leinie Lodge

Grilling with Beer at the Leinie's Family Reunion, Chippewa Falls, WI

Generations of families gathered with their friends for the third annual Family Reunion and BBQ at the Leinie Lodge in Chippewa Falls. With more than 3,000 people attending the one-day event, it was a fest for food, family, friends and a fabulous shopping spree on the day before Father's Day.

Yup, in a single afternoon, more than half the attendees swarmed through the gift shop in the Leinie Lodge, to find souvenirs and gifts for Father's Day. The outdoorsmen hunted and the womenfolk gathered, shopping for Leinie-brand muskie lures, fishing poles, hunter's knifes, baseball caps, canoe paddles, tents, duffel bags, sweat pants, shorts, T-shirts, umbrellas, vests, jackets, aprons, oven mitts, ice chests and coolers, pint glasses, even beer soap.

Hundreds stood in line to have those souvenirs signed by the three Leinenkugel brothers—Jake, Dick, and John. Families posed for pictures

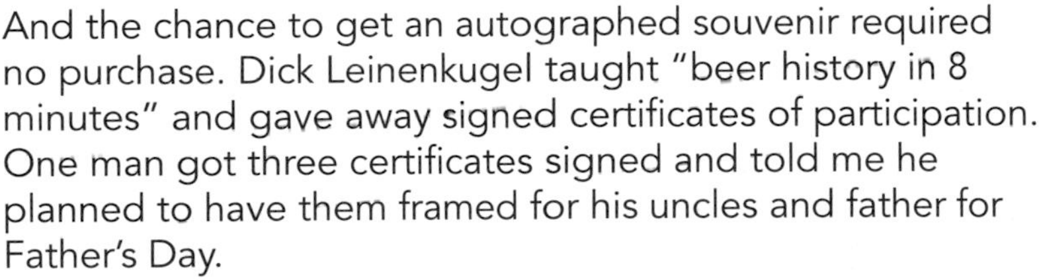

in the giant Leinie Lounger Adirondack chair.

Beyond the bonanza of free pint glasses for the first 100 attendees, there were free bratwurst and food for all.

The turkey brats (donated by Jennie-O) were cooked over the grill and then warmed in a special beer and onion mixture. Cookies and root beer tempted the young ones, while the older folks (with proof of age) got wrist bracelets with tags for 3 free glasses of beer.

And the chance to get an autographed souvenir required no purchase. Dick Leinenkugel taught "beer history in 8 minutes" and gave away signed certificates of participation. One man got three certificates signed and told me he planned to have them framed for his uncles and father for Father's Day.

But I was there (as a writer and as a judge) for the food. A cook-off featuring two dueling chefs was organized by Peggy Leinenkugel, avid cook, recipe creator and wife of Jake. Toni Fladmark, publisher of *Cabin Life* magazine, drove in from Duluth, Minnesota to serve as a judge, along with the throngs of taste-testers who submitted their votes for People's Choice.

Cabin Life magazine is a big fan of the Jacob Leinenkugel Brewery, and the only consumer magazine to offer a recipe competition specifically for grilling with beer. Last year, *Cabin Life* and the Leinenkugel brothers kicked off "The Grill Master Grilling with Beer" competition with a bratwurst cookout. Prizes for the best grilling with beer recipes included Leinie's gear and a Ducane gas grill.

The Family Reunion competition pitted the quintessential tavern cook, Deano Tinjum of Deano's Big Ten Tap, against the talented bistro chefs from Mona Lisa's, vying for the title of Chef Leinie's. The rules for entry, set by Peggy Leinenkugel, required that Leinie's be used as an ingredient at some phase of the preparation and that the recipe be prepared outdoors, using standard camping cookout gear. That's in keeping with the brewery's tagline, "the Flavor of the Northwoods."

Recipes ranged from grilled pork loin to smoked salmon with honey weiss mustard sauce and a salad of mixed mesclun lettuce garnished with fresh raspberries and dried Wisconsin cranberries.

"A backyard BBQ in a bowl," the Easy Chili by Deano featured diced smoked chicken, sliced cooked brats and chopped grilled burgers in a smooth tomato-y base, without a lot of chilies or spices. The grilled pork loin marinated in Leinie's Red turned out perfectly, with a nice pink smoke ring and still juicy and tender inside.

Participating chef Tim also basted grilled chicken with a blend of beer and chopped tomatoes with green chilies.

Chef Jeno and owner Lisa Aspenson of Mona Lisa's created a more elaborate dish, with Three Leinies Smoked Salmon. The salmon was marinated in the Red Lager, smoked over wood chips soaked in the Original Lager, and served with a mustard sauce made with the Honey Weiss.

Though the Easy Chili took home the People's Choice award for top taste, I liked the smoked salmon so much that Mona Lisa's agreed to share the recipe. —L.S.

Mona Lisa's Three Leinie's Smoked Salmon

Equipment needed: Charcoal smoker, propane camp stove, charcoal or fuel, 2 cups hickory wood chips for smoking, small saucepan

- 24 ounces red lager
- 12 ounces pilsner lager
- 1 large filet Atlantic salmon
- 2 tablespoons fresh dill weed
- Sea salt and freshly ground black pepper
- 1 bottle honey weiss
- 2 tablespoons minced shallots or onions
- 2 tablespoons olive oil
- 3 tablespoons stone-ground grainy mustard
- 3 tablespoons prepared Dijon mustard
- Honey, to taste

1. Soak hickory chips in lager. Marinate salmon in enough red lager to cover, and sprinkle with dill; chill for 1½ hours. Remove salmon from marinade and season generously with salt and pepper. Fill smoker with charcoal and light the fire. When the coals are hot, drain the wood chips and add them to the coals. Immediately place salmon in smoker and smoked for 1 to 1½ hours, depending on thickness of filet, until fish is firm to the touch. Remove salmon from smoker. Prepare sauce and serve as shown.

2. Place shallots or onion in olive oil in a small saucepan on your portable propane camp stove, set to medium-low heat. Cook and stir shallots until just tender, add the honey weiss and reduce to about 1 cup. Add the remaining ingredients and cook until thickened. Serve over salmon with salad, toast or crackers.

Yields 6 to 8 servings.

Burgers, Chops & Steaks

Sure, they're the usual suspects in any BBQ line-up, but burgers, chops and steaks taste even better with craft beer. The big malty flavors enhance the caramelization of meat on the grill. Even turkey burgers get a boost in taste from craft brew.

Burgers are simple to make when using store-bought ground beef. But as a home cook, you have better control over quality and freshness by making your own ground meats. Start with a slab of steak or well-trimmed chuck. Or, make ground turkey from boneless breast meat, and not scads of fatty skin. Any moisture you add comes from craft beer, not a saline solution designed to preserve shelf life.

So, roll up your sleeves and wash your hands. Trim away visible fat, remove any leftover bones and gristle, and place meat in the freezer for 15 minutes. Cut meat into 1-inch cubes, and place in food processor fitted with the chopping blade. Process only 2 cups at a time, and pulse for 2 seconds just 6 times, stopping and scraping sides of bowl once. Do not overprocess, or the meat will be mushy. Scrape ground meat into a bowl and repeat until all meat is chopped. Mix well and chill until ready to prepare one of the following beer burger recipes. This little bit of effort is well worth the better taste.

Brewer's Burgers

I have a large bay leaf plant, which yields plenty of fresh leaves. You can also buy fresh bay leaves at most grocery stores.

- 6 fresh bay leaves
- 2 tablespoons sea salt
- 24 ounces amber lager
- 2 pounds chuck, trimmed, cut into 2-inch chunks
- 1 tablespoon cracked black pepper
- 2 tablespoons minced garlic
- 2 dashes Worcestershire sauce
- ¼ cup panko bread crumbs
- Salt and pepper to taste

1. Put bay leaves and salt in large glass bowl, and crush with back of a wooden spoon until salt turns aromatic. Do not chop bay leaves.

2. Mix lager, meat, pepper, garlic and Worcestershire sauce in same bowl with bay leaves and salt; cover and chill overnight. Drain beef with sieve, remove and discard bay leaves, and coarsely grind using ¼-inch setting on a meat grinder, or chop in small batches in food processor (do not over-mince). Knead in bread crumbs until well mixed and chill 1 hour.

3. Prepare grill to medium heat. Form large ¼-pound patties, sprinkle with salt and pepper and grill until medium-rare, about 8 minutes per side.

Makes 8 servings.

Tip: You can double this recipe and reserve half the ground meat for later use. Just wrap and freeze, and when ready to cook, thaw and add breadcrumbs.

Brewer's Burgers

Asian Lager Burgers

- 1 pound ground turkey
- 1 tablespoon soy sauce
- ¼ cup Asian dry lager
- ¼ cup panko bread crumbs
- 2 tablespoons chopped lemongrass bulb (tender white part only)
- 1 tablespoon Asian chile sauce such as Sriracha
- 2 tablespoons minced scallions (green leaves)

1. Mix turkey, soy sauce and lager in medium bowl. Set aside. In a food processor fitted with the metal chopping blade, pulse bread crumbs and lemongrass until lemongrass is very finely minced. Knead this mixture into turkey blend, and add chile sauce and scallions.

2. Cover meat mixture and chill 1 hour. Prepare grill. Form meat into 4 to 6 patties and grill over indirect heat.

Makes 4 to 6 servings.

Note: Panko bread crumbs are light, fluffy bread crumbs originally developed in Japan, and most often used for extra-crispy tempura crusts. The light texture soaks up flavors without turning heavy.

beerbistro Lamb Burgers

- 2¼ pounds lean ground lamb (regular grind)
- 3 to 4 slices Italian or other crusty bread
- 1 whole egg
- ¼ cup minced onion
- 1 tablespoon minced garlic
- 1 cup English mild ale or lightly hopped amber ale
- 2 tablespoons Dijon mustard
- 2 tablespoons ketchup
- 1 tablespoon fresh minced rosemary
- 1 tablespoon fresh minced basil
- 2 tablespoons fresh minced parsley
- 1 teaspoon hot Tabasco sauce
- ¼ teaspoon Worcestershire sauce
- 2 teaspoons salt
- ½ teaspoon ground black pepper

1. Tear 3 slices Italian or crusty bread into pieces and place in blender or food processor. Pulse until fine to yield 1 cup crumbs. Pour crumbs into large nonreactive mixing bowl. Place remaining ingredients in bowl and knead well, until evenly mixed. Cover and chill overnight to allow beef to absorb beer and flavorings.
2. Portion meat into 6-ounce balls and form patties. These will seem a little soft, but will firm up on grill while remaining juicy inside.
3. Prepare grill; once coals are ready or gas grill is preheated, brush grilling rack with a little oil. Place burgers on grill and cook 4 minutes, or until firm, before turning them. Turn burgers only once on grill and do not squish with a spatula. Burgers should take about 4 minutes per side on a medium-hot grill. Serve as soon as possible on toasted buns.

Makes 8 servings.

TropicAle Pork Chops

- ½ cup unsweetened pineapple juice
- 12 ounces witbier
- 1 tablespoon minced garlic
- 2 tablespoons minced candied ginger or 2 tablespoons grated ginger
- 1 tablespoon brown sugar
- 1 to 2 habañero peppers, seeded and minced
- ⅓ cup chopped chives
- 1 tablespoon diced pimiento
- 2 tablespoons lime juice
- 1 tablespoon dark rum
- 1 teaspoon salt
- 1½ teaspoons ground black pepper
- 2 pounds pork chops

1. Place juice, witbier, garlic, ginger and brown sugar in saucepan over low heat; simmer until reduced by one-fourth, about 10 minutes. Cool and mix with peppers, chives, pimiento, lime juice, rum, salt and pepper. Reserve ½ cup mixture.

2. Place pork in large resealable plastic bag and cover with remaining marinade. Seal and chill at least 2 hours or overnight for best flavor. Prepare grill to medium heat. Grill over indirect heat (use foil if necessary to prevent flare-ups). When done, remove from heat and serve with rice salad drizzled with reserved marinade.

Makes 4 to 6 servings.

TropicAle Pork Chops

Mt. Tam Pale Ale Marinated T-Bone Steaks

Jenn Kolthoff of the Marin Brewing Co. shares a recipe for grilled steaks featured at the BBQ and beer fundraiser for the Charlotte Maxwell Clinic's breast cancer treatment programs, aptly called "The Breast Fest."

- 4 cups pale ale
- ¾ cups minced garlic
- ½ cup beef stock
- 1 cup olive oil
- ½ cup fresh chopped rosemary
- ½ cup fresh chopped thyme
- 3 tablespoons paprika
- 2 tablespoons salt (or to taste)
- 2 tablespoons black pepper
- 2 tablespoons red chili pepper flakes
- 8 well-trimmed T-bone steaks (10 ounces each)

1. Combine all ingredients, except steak, in large shallow casserole dish. Fit steaks in dish with marinade, cover with plastic wrap and chill at least 6 hours, turning steaks twice to marinade evenly.

2. Remove steaks from marinade and let rest 1 hour at room temperature. Meanwhile, prepare grill to medium heat. Grill steaks on both sides, rotating twice for p.g.m. (pretty grill marks). Cook 6 to 10 minutes on each side (depending on thickness of cut), and let rest on a warm platter for 5 minutes before serving.

Makes 8 servings.

India Pale Ale (IPA) Marinated Skirt Steaks

Here's another spicy steak from the Marin Brewing Co., prepared at the BBQ and beer fundraiser for the Charlotte Maxwell Clinic's breast cancer treatment, called "Fermenting Change: Microbreweries Battling Breast Cancer."

- 4 cups India Pale Ale
- ¼ cup minced garlic
- ½ cup Chinese black bean garlic sauce
- ½ cup hoisin sauce
- ½ cup olive oil
- 1 cup chopped green onions
- 2 tablespoons salt
- 2 tablespoons ground black pepper
- 2 tablespoons paprika
- 3 pounds trimmed skirt steak

1. Combine all ingredients, except steak, in large shallow casserole dish. Fit steaks in dish with marinade, cover with plastic wrap and chill at least 6 hours, turning steaks twice to marinade evenly.

2. Remove steaks from marinade and let rest 1 hour at room temperature. Meanwhile prepare grill to medium heat. Grill steaks on both sides, rotating twice for p.g.m. (pretty grill marks). Cook 6 to 8 minutes on each side (depending on thickness of cut), and let rest on a warm platter for 5 minutes before serving.

Makes 4 to 6 servings.

Adobo Dark Lager Burgers

- 8 ounces Mexican dark lager
- ½ cup masa harina or corn flour
- 3 pounds ground chuck, ¼-inch grind is best
- 2 tablespoons sauce from chipotles en adobo
- ¼ cup finely minced cilantro
- ¼ cup finely minced Serrano pepper
- 1 teaspoon salt
- 1 teaspoon ground black pepper

1. In a large bowl, mix together all ingredients, except salt and pepper. Cover and chill overnight or at least 4 hours. Form 12 burger patties and sprinkle with salt and pepper. Chill at least 1 hour to set.

2. Prepare grill. Cook patties over medium-high heat, flipping just once (burgers are tender and may fall part). Serve with Roasted Corn Salsa (recipe follows).

Makes 12 servings.

Roasted Corn Salsa

- 4 ears roasted corn
- 1 cup chopped Bermuda red onion
- ⅓ cup minced parsley
- 1 cup finely chopped cherry or grape tomatoes
- 1 cup finely chopped green bell pepper
- 2 tablespoons lime juice
- 1 tablespoon soy sauce
- 1 tablespoon canola oil
- Pinch cayenne pepper

1. Cut kernels off roasted corn to yield 4 cups. Place kernels in large glass bowl and add remaining ingredients. Toss to mix.

Makes 12 servings (½ cup portion).

Adobo Dark Lager Burgers

Redeye Ribeye Steaks

- 12 ounces dark lager
- 2 tablespoons minced garlic
- ¼ cup minced red onion
- 1 teaspoon hot pepper sauce
- 2 tablespoons grapefruit juice
- ¼ cup molasses
- 2 tablespoons brown or spicy prepared mustard
- 2 tablespoons olive oil
- 6 well-trimmed ribeye steaks (approximately 8 oz. each)
- 2 teaspoons salt
- 2 teaspoons coarsely ground black pepper
- 2 teaspoons dark brown sugar

1. Blend lager, garlic, onion, pepper sauce, grapefruit juice, molasses, mustard and olive oil in blender on HIGH until smooth. Reserve ¼ cup for basting, and pour remaining marinade over steaks in a large shallow dish. Cover and chill at least 2 hours, turning steaks once to marinade on both sides.

2. Mix salt, pepper and brown sugar to make a spice rub. Remove steaks from marinade and sprinkle with spice rub. Press rub into surface of meat. Prepare grill to medium-high heat. Grill steaks over indirect heat, about 5 minutes per side (depending on thickness of cut). Baste with reserved marinade.

3. Remove steaks from grill and let rest 5 minutes on warm platter before serving.

Makes 6 servings.

Pecan-Pale Ale Lamb

- ⅓ cup pecans
- 1 tablespoon coriander seeds
- 2 cloves garlic, peeled
- 1 tablespoon olive oil
- 8 ounces pale ale
- ½ teaspoon red pepper flakes
- 1 teaspoon salt
- 1½ to 2 pounds lamb chops or lamb shoulder steaks

1. In blender, blend all ingredients except lamb on HIGH to an emulsion. Remove ¼ cup and set aside.
Pour remainder into resealable plastic bag. Add lamb and marinate at least 2 hours.

2. Prepare grill or broiler to medium heat and cook lamb to medium-rare (or desired doneness). Remove from heat and let stand 5 minutes before slicing. Drizzle with reserved pecan ale mixture.

Makes 6 to 8 servings.

Brats In Beer

It's the soul food of Wisconsin, or so claims the Bratwurst Page, a site created by Jim Schroeder that is devoted to the gustatory pleasures of the Badger State. Brats cooked in beer offer sustenance for tailgates, picnics, barbecues and all kinds of parties. There's even a Bratwurst Hall of Fame in Sheboygan, Wisconsin.

Although most Wisconsin natives know that bratwurst should be cooked in pale, fizzy pilsner-style lagers or, as Schroeder advises, "the cheapest beer available," I ventured into new territory by simmering brats in craft beers. Always the subversive chef, I tried adding spices and other sauces, which are strictly verboten, according to Schroeder.

"Just use beer and onions," says Schroeder. "There's no need for anything else."

The basic technique for grilling beer brats is to slowly heat the brats in beer in a large pan set over the grill. Though some people talk about boiling brats in beer, actually letting the beer come to a rolling boil is awful treatment for the tender fresh wursts. Boiled brats will burst out of their casings, and that's an ugly sight. Such cruelty to encased meats can be avoided. The best treatment is a very hot bath in beer, with just a few wisps of steam to show the heat is still going.

After about 20 minutes in the hot beer bath, the brats turn a milky-gray color. Use tongs to place the brats on the grill over medium heat. Avoid piercing the casings, or the juices will run out. How hot should the grill be? Schroeder says, "A good test is to hold your hand, palm down, 2 inches above the grate. If you can hold it there for 4 to 5 seconds, the coals are just right. If you can still see a red glow, it's too early to start cooking."

Rotate the brats often on the grill. One bratmeister I know uses his bare hands to rotate the brats, but I prefer tongs. The brats should brown for at least 10 minutes before serving. You can serve the brat hot and crisp-browned from the grill. Or, if serving a crowd, make a holding sauce of more beer, onions and a few tablespoons of butter. If you put the grilled brats in a holding sauce, the casings turn soft and some of the juices leach into the sauce.

"In Sheboygan, they are persnickety about what you put on a brat," says Schroeder. "Raw onion, brown mustard, pickles and two brats on a round hard roll side by side. That's it, although there are heretics even in Sheboygan who use ketchup." Elsewhere, brats are bedecked in sauerkraut, ketchup, barbecue sauce and even yellow mustard.

Some brat-makers think that the beer bath spoils the taste of the meat by making it bitter, and dilutes the seasonings so carefully added to the sausages. So, if cooking brats in beer isn't appropriate for your guests, or to your taste, try the grilled beer onions. The topping will add the taste of beer for just those who appreciate it.

Here are recipes to prepare bratwurst (or even chicken sausages) in craft beer, with ingredients bound to surprise a bratmeister, but delicious nonetheless.

Custer's Bold Beer Brats

A great cook and generous recipe tester, Lee Custer enjoys cooking outdoors over real wood, sometimes in a grill and sometimes over open fires. Here's his riff on the best brats.

- 4 or more fresh bratwursts
- 1 sliced onion for every 4 brats
- 1 clove garlic for every 4 brats
- Ale or lager to cover brats, at least 12 ounces
- 1 teaspoon hot sauce, or more to taste
- Spicy brown mustard

1. Place brats in medium saucepan over low heat; add onions, garlic and beer. Simmer 20 minutes. Remove brats from simmering beer and reserve cooking liquid in pot over low heat. Place brats on prepared grill to brown.

2. Place brats back in warm beer and onion mixture. Cook on grill over medium heat 15 to 20 minutes. Serve with hot sauce and strained onions and garlic on oversized buns with plenty of spicy brown mustard.

Makes 4 or more servings.

Herbed Ale Brats

8 fresh bratwursts
2 bottles (24 ounces) pale ale (not too hoppy)
⅓ cup minced onion
1 tablespoon flour
3 tablespoons butter
2 tablespoons dill pickle relish
1 tablespoon minced garlic
1 tablespoon minced parsley
1 tablespoon minced marjoram
1 teaspoon salt
1 teaspoon freshly ground black pepper
Spicy brown mustard

1. Simmer brats with 14 to 16 ounces pale ale (just enough to cover) and onion in deep skillet placed over hot grill. After 20 minutes, remove from beer and place brats on grill to brown. Discard beer and onions used to cook brats.

2. In medium saucepan, whisk and sauté flour and butter over medium heat until a roux forms (light brown paste). Slowly whisk in 1 cup pale ale, and simmer 2 minutes. Whisk until smooth. Stir in relish, garlic, parsley, marjoram, salt and pepper. Simmer, stirring often, until sauce is thickened.

3. Dip and roll brats in herb sauce and serve on toasted or grilled buns with spicy brown mustard and desired garnishes.

Makes 8 servings.

Herbed Ale Brats

Robust Rosemary Beer Mustard

- ¼ cup brown mustard seeds
- ¼ cup yellow mustard seeds
- ¾ cup pale ale
- 1 tablespoon ground mustard
- 2 tablespoons minced scallions
- 2 tablespoons minced rosemary
- ⅓ cup cider vinegar
- 2 tablespoons dark brown sugar
- 1 teaspoon salt

1. Soak mustard seeds in ale overnight. When seeds are soft, place ale-seed mixture in blender or food processor with remaining ingredients. Blend or process on HIGH until a paste forms, with some seeds remaining whole. Scrape mixture into sterile glass jar, cover and refrigerate 4 to 5 days before using. Use within 3 weeks.

Makes about 1¼ cups.

Amber Ale Brats with Onion & Sauerkraut

- 8 fresh bratwursts
- 2 bottles (24 ounces) malty amber ale
- 1 tablespoon minced garlic
- 2 cups sauerkraut
- 2 large yellow onions, peeled and sliced
- 2 tablespoons applesauce
- 1 to 2 teaspoons fennel seed (to taste)
- 1 teaspoon ground black pepper, or more to taste
- 1 tablespoon molasses
- Dijon mustard

1. Simmer brats with 14 to 16 ounces amber ale (just enough to cover) and minced garlic in deep skillet placed over hot grill. After 20 minutes, remove from beer and place brats on grill to brown.

2. Mix remaining amber ale, sauerkraut, onions, applesauce, fennel seed, pepper and molasses in skillet placed over medium heat. Simmer uncovered until most of ale has reduced and onions are very soft. Serve brats on toasted or grilled buns with Dijon mustard, topped with several spoonfuls of well-drained sauerkraut and onion mixture.

Makes 8 servings.

Gold and Green Brats

- 8 fresh bratwursts
- 16 ounces amber ale or chipotle ale, for a spicier taste
- 1 tablespoon minced garlic
- 1 yellow bell pepper
- 1 green bell pepper
- ½ cup minced onion
- 1 teaspoon thyme
- 1 teaspoon kosher salt
- 1 teaspoon red pepper flakes
- 1 tablespoon olive oil

1. Simmer brats with 14 to 16 ounces amber ale (just enough to cover) and minced garlic in deep skillet placed on hot grill or side burner over medium heat.

2. Prepare large sheet of heavy-duty foil by spraying it with nonstick cooking spray. Slice and core peppers and toss with onion, thyme, salt, red pepper flakes and olive oil. Mound vegetable mixture on foil and roll up edges, crimping to seal. Place foil pack on grill.

3. After 20 minutes in ale and garlic mixture, remove brats from beer and place on grill to brown. Turn foil pack several times. When brats are browned, carefully slide foil pack onto a platter and use tongs to unroll foil. Let a corner open first and stand back to avoid steam hitting your face or hands. Serve brats with a spoonful of yellow and green pepper mixture on toasted buns.

Makes 8 servings.

Gold and Green Brats

Stout Spiced Brats

- 8 fresh bratwursts
- 2 bottles (12 ounces each) stout or dark lager of choice
- 2 tablespoons minced onion
- ½ cup prepared Dijon mustard
- 2 tablespoons molasses
- 1 tablespoon Worcestershire sauce
- ½ teaspoon ground nutmeg
- ¼ teaspoon ground cloves
- Pinch ground white pepper

1. Simmer brats with 12 to 16 ounces stout (enough to cover) and onion in deep pan over medium heat. After 20 minutes, remove brats from stout and place on grill to brown.

2. Add mustard, molasses, Worcestershire sauce, nutmeg and cloves to stout mixture. Simmer in skillet until thickened and reduced by half. Dip and roll brats in sauce before placing on buns and serving. Serve with additional stout or barley wine.

Makes 8 servings.

Basic Bratology

Q Why discard the onions and beer used to cook brats?

A It's your call, actually. I don't like the gray smidgens of brat bits that float in the beer, but many people adore the taste. Some cooks even use the brat-beer simmer liquid as the base for a bean soup or stew instead of stock.

Summertime Brats

Several American craft brewers, such as the Saint Arnold Brewing Co. of Houston, Texas, and the Goose Island Brewery of Chicago, Illinois, make summer seasonal ales in the Kölsch style.

- 2 tablespoons butter
- 2 cups sliced onion
- 12 ounces kölsch beer
- 1 teaspoon caraway seeds (or more, according to taste)
- 1 tablespoon brown mustard seeds
- 1 to 2 teaspoons freshly ground black pepper, divided (or according to taste)
- 6 to 8 fresh bratwurts
- ½ cup minced scallion
- ½ cup diced tomato
- 1 teaspoon salt

1. Mix butter, onion, kolsch, caraway, mustard seeds and pepper in large pot set over hot grill. Add brats and bring to a simmer. After 20 minutes, remove brats from kolsch and place on grill to brown.

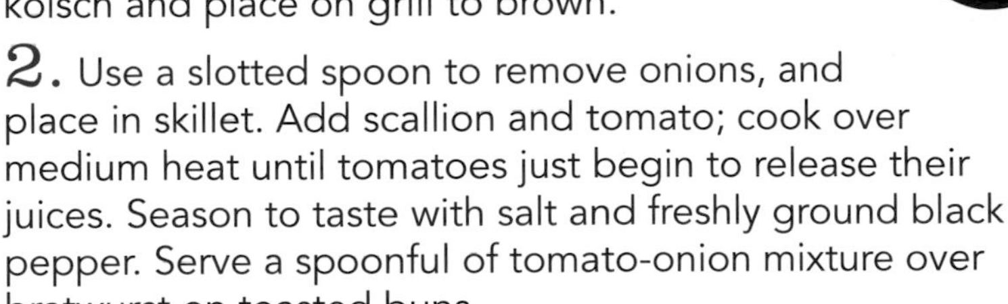

2. Use a slotted spoon to remove onions, and place in skillet. Add scallion and tomato; cook over medium heat until tomatoes just begin to release their juices. Season to taste with salt and freshly ground black pepper. Serve a spoonful of tomato-onion mixture over bratwurst on toasted buns.

Makes 6 to 8 servings.

Grilled Beer Onions

Eric Nielsen, brewer and craft beer consultant, suggests adding a teaspoon of molasses and a dusting of nutritional yeast to the canola oil. "This will enhance the Maillard reaction, which cranks out fantastic caramel taste and color."

- 5 to 6 very large Spanish onions, peeled and cut into ⅓-inch slices
- ¼ cup canola oil
- 1 teaspoon molasses
- ½ teaspoon nutritional brewer's yeast
- 1 teaspoon celery seeds
- 1 tablespoon brown mustard seeds
- 1 teaspoon dry powdered mustard (or more to taste)
- 2 teaspoons sugar
- 1 teaspoon salt
- 1 teaspoon ground black pepper
- 12 ounces brown ale or rauchbier
- 2 teaspoons cornstarch or potato starch

1. Place onion slices on large cookie sheet and drizzle with oil to coat evenly. Place on grill and cook, turning twice, until just tender and grill marks are brown on both sides.

2. Mix celery seeds, mustard seeds, mustard, sugar, salt, pepper, ale and cornstarch in blender on HIGH until smooth. Place 12-inch cast iron skillet on grill. Place onions and ale mixture in skillet and stir to coat onions evenly. Cook 15 minutes, stirring often, until beer glaze is thick and onions are soft. May make 24 hours in advance (beer flavor will intensify).

Makes 4 to 5 cups.

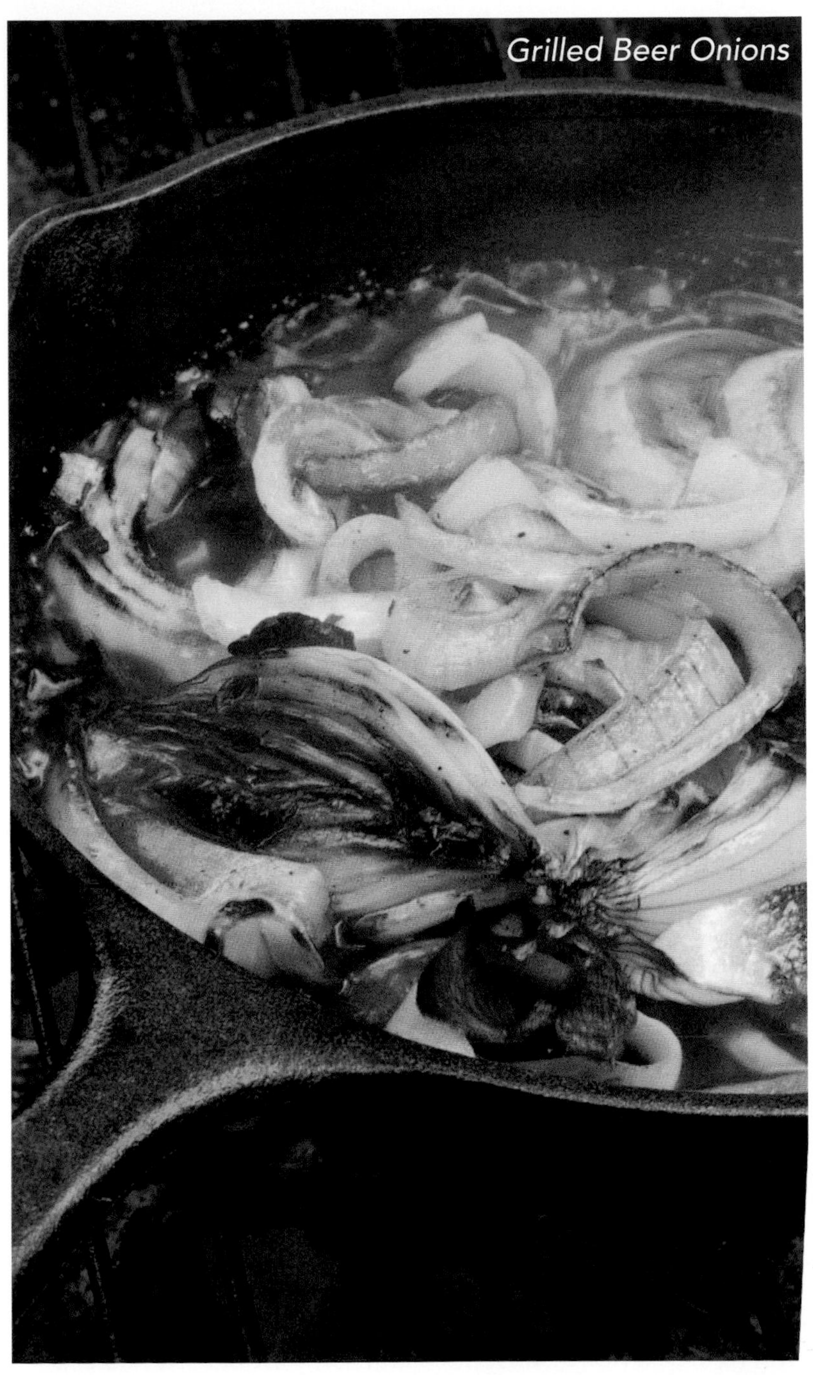
Grilled Beer Onions

Appendix I:

Match Points

by Stan Hieronymus

www.appellationbeer.com

The last thing you want when you're cooking over hot coals, getting ready to put food on the table, and picking a beer to drink, is *complicated.*

It's grilling. We're outside. It's beer. This should be fun.

Recent chatter that craft beer is the "new wine," the realization that beer deserves a place at the table, and a growing list of handy pairing rules in magazines and newspaper columns may leave you feeling that the once simple act of putting a pint of beer by a plate has become, well, *complicated.*

Worrying about finding the perfect match shouldn't ruin a meal, because when you start with a favorite dish and a favorite beer you often needn't consider anything else. If you want to think a little more about pairing, then use Lucy's straightforward suggestions on pages 19-20.

And a little more? Consider the "three Cs" that Lucy first introduced us to in Cooking with Beer, published in 1995. These are "cut," "complement" and "contrast." For instance, if you spice up the Smoked Ale Mustard Sauce (page 30) you might choose a hoppy American IPA to cut the heat and the smoke. You could be just as happy serving the smoked beer you used in the sauce to complement a piece of beef slathered in the sauce.

Contrast is not as simple as looking to opposites. Think in terms of the intensity and complexity of flavors in both the dish and the beer. An American pale ale may contrast nicely with hearty, smoky barbecue but it only works if it has the heft to stand up to the dish.

Beer's versatility—sweetness from malt, bitterness from hops, the cleansing ability of carbonation—makes pairing easier, but not foolproof. You won't appreciate the delicate nuances of grilled shrimp if you pair the dish with something intense like a robust porter. Common sense will keep you from some disasters, while experimenting and keeping a list of your successes and favorite flavors should keep you from duplicating "mis-tastes."

Here's a way to experiment at your next grilling get-together.

For the main dish, use the Tamarind Amber Glaze (page 70) to grill both salmon and shrimp.

For the sides, prepare both the Brined Grilled Eggplant (page 166) and use the Tarragon IPA Brine (page 116) on more eggplant.

You should already have an amber ale, a strong golden and an American IPA that you used in the recipes. Add a German weiss beer, a Belgian White, a Belgian saison and a dark lager (or German dunkel).

Try tastes of each of the dishes, with sips of all seven beers. With 28 possible combinations, you should find plenty of pairings. Which beers overwhelm the shrimp? Which best complement the salmon? How do the grilled vegetables compare when you try them first with the strong golden, then with the saison and finally with the IPA? Why? When does the taste of spices in a glaze, brine, marinade or sauce become more important? When does the underlying flavor of the main ingredient matter more? And how about when you take into consideration side dishes as well as main dishes?

The best answers are your own answers. Focus on the refreshing flavors of craft beer—remember, nothing too *complicated*. —Stan Hieronymus

Appendix II: Mail Order Resources

Asian Ingredients

Bead molasses, panko bread crumbs, black bean chili paste, toasted sesame oil and other Asian ingredients called for in GRILLING WITH BEER can be found online or via telephone mail order here.

AsianFoodGrocer.com

Toll Free: 888-482-2742
Phone: 650-873-7600 ext 107
Fax: 650-871-9154

Address:
131 West Harris Avenue
San Francisco, CA 94080, US

Email: info@asianfoodgrocer.com

The Oriental Pantry
www.orientalpantry.com

Phone: 978-264-4576
Fax: 781-275-4506

Address:

423 Great Road (2A)
Acton, MA 01720

Email through a contact form on the website

Chiles, Herbs, & Spices

Guajillo, ajillo and other chiles, plus whole or ground spices, can be found via mail order and online through several sources. I've ordered from MoHotta MoBetta, the Spice House and Vann's and been pleased with the selections. MoHotta also has lots of pepper sauces, if you don't want to handle raw or dried chiles.

MoHotta MoBetta
www.mohotta.com.

Phone 800-462-3220
Fax 800-618-4454 or 912-748-1364
International 912-748-2766

Address:
P.O. Box 1026
Savannah, GA 31402 USA

Email mohotta@mohotta.com

The Spice House
www.thespicehouse.com

Phone: 414-272-0977
Fax: 414-272-1271

Address:
1031 North Old World Third Street,
Milwaukee, Wisconsin 53203 USA

Email through a contact form
on the website

Vann's Spices Ltd.
www.vannsspices.com

Phone: 410-358-3007
Fax: 410-358-1780
Toll Free Phone: 800-583-1693
Toll Free FAX: 800-358-1617

Address:
6105 Oakleaf Avenue
Baltimore, Maryland 21215 USA

sales@vannsspices.com

Specialty Meats

Several online retailers will ship meats and poultry.

For natural beef, lamb and pork:

Niman Ranch
www.nimanranch.com

Phone: 866-808-0340
Fax: 510-808-0339

Address:
1025 E. 12th St.
Oakland, CA 94606

Email: info@nimanranch.com

For organic beef:

www.davismountains organicbeef.com

Phone: 1-877-366-2333
Fax: 972-265-0290

Address:
5601 Democracy Drive, Suite 190
Plano, TX 75024

For natural lamb and lamb sausages:

Jamison Farm
www.jamisonfarm.com

Toll Free: 1-800-237-5262
Fax: 1-724-837-2287

Address:
171 Jamison Lane
Latrobe, PA 15650

E-mail: john@jamisonfarm.com

Mail Order Beer

Laws governing shipment of beer vary from state to state in the US, and seem to change from month to month. An experienced retailer can guide your selection.
John's Grocery is one of the leading retailers of craft beer and one of the few that will ship beer based on your own personal choices.

John's Grocery Inc.
www.johnsgrocery.com

Phone: 319.337.2183
Fax: 319.339.4904

Address:
401 E. Market St.
Iowa City, IA 52245

Email through a contact form
on the website

For a "beer of the month" selection of unusual imported beers and American craft brews, chosen by Michael Jackson of the Beer Hunter series:

http://rarebeerclub.beveragebistro.com

Phone: 888-380-2337
Fax: 425-861-8522

Address:
17530 N.E. Union Hill Road
Suite 150
Redmond, WA 98052 USA

Email through a contact form on the website

Mail Order Bratwursts

Brats made in Wisconsin include several companies, from giant Johnsonville to the Bavarian Sausage Co. of Madison, Wisconsin, which makes bratwurst with craft beer from the local JT Whitney's Pub.

Johnsonville Brats
www.johnsonville.com

Phone: 888-556-BRAT

Address:
P.O. Box 906
Sheboygan Falls, WI 53085

Email through a contact form on the website

Fred Usinger, Inc.
www.usinger.com

Phone: (414) 276-9100
Gifts: (414) 276-9105
Toll Free: (800) 558-9998
Fax: (414) 291-5277

Address:
1030 N. Old World Third Street
Milwaukee Wisconsin, 53203 USA

Email: info@usinger.com

Bavaria Sausage, Inc.
www.bavariasausage.com

Phone: 608-271-1295
Toll Free: 1-800-733-6695
Fax: 608-845-6693

Address:
6317 Nesbitt Road
Madison, WI 53719 USA

Email: sales@bavariasausage.com

Barley Malt Extract

Eden Foods sells barley malt extract made from USA organically grown barley, sprouted, kiln roasted, and slowly cooked into a thick, dark brown syrup—an ancient process using only the grain's own enzymes created in the sprouting process, and the knowledge and care of artisan maltsters. A rich mellow flavor that's half as sweet as refined sugar and ideal for barbecue sauces made with beer. Eden Foods also sells soy sauces and oils.

Eden Foods
www.edenfoods.com/store

Phone: 517-456-7424
Fax: 517-456-7025

Address:
701 Tecumseh Road
Clinton, Michigan 49236

E-Mail: websales@edenfoods.com

Appendix III: Flavors of Craft Beer

Throughout this book, I offer suggestions for specific beer styles to be used in recipes. If you don't know how the taste of a porter differs from a pilsner, please read this section.

This appendix offers resources for educating yourself and short descriptions of the cookbook's most frequently used beer styles and their dominant flavors.

Entire books are devoted to beer styles, such as Michael Jackson's Beer Companion: The World's Great Beer Styles, Gastronomy, and Traditions (Running Press, 2000), Stephen Beaumont's Premium Beer Drinkers Guide (Firefly Books, 2000) and Ray Daniel's Designing Great Beers (Brewers Association, 2000). With literally thousands of brands of beer available, it's difficult to name brand names for each beer style available in all states, countries, and seasons. To locate specific styles and brands, check out the databases online at BeerAdvocate.com, RateBeer.com or RealBeer.com, where members are often very helpful with suggestions and ratings.

If you are intrigued by beer styles and want to visit a brewery, the Brewers Association website, beertown.org, offers a searchable database of craft breweries by location, as does Bill Metzger's brewingnews.com. Stephen Beaumont (worldofbeer.com) is also the author of The Great Canadian Beer Guide (McArthur Books, 2001). In the UK, the Campaign for Real Ale (camra.org) offers guides to the UK and European breweries. Chances are, you can find one nearby that offers tours. One of the most enjoyable (and typically affordable) ways to taste new styles of beer is to go on a brewery tour.

One excellent way to quickly taste more styles of beer is to attend beer festivals; beerfestivals.org lists events around the world where beer tasting is celebrated. Magazines and brewspapers such as *All About Beer*, *Ale Street News*, *Brewing News*, the *Celebrator*, *DRAFT* and *Imbibe*, offer reviews of new brands and festivals. The Great American Beer Festival (beertown.org) and the Great Canadian Beer Festival (gcbf.com) are two of the biggest festivals, spanning several days.

To learn more about beer styles, the Brewers Association offers style guidelines used to judge beer at professional competitions. The Beer Judge Certification Program, bjcp.org, offers training and a guide to styles online.

Another resource is the Essential Reference of Domestic Brewers and Their Bottled Brands.
The book and its companion website offer a comprehensive annual reference of all domestically available bottled beer brands and their producers. Listings are shown alphabetically, by color and bitterness charts, by beer style, by distribution area, by geographic location, and by brewery. The Bitterness Comparison Charts are particularly helpful to show the gradations of hoppiness by IBUs (International Bittering Units). Purchase of the book, available at www.essentialbeerreference.com, includes website access to track updates and seasonal releases.

Bear in mind that taste is subjective. My idea of "floral and fruity" may not match yours. That is why I urge you to sample (in moderation) many different brands and styles of beer. You'll find the ones that please you, and those should be your top choice at the table or in the kitchen. Keep in mind that kitchen and table beers not be same styles; I personally don't much enjoy drinking rauchbier straight, but couldn't live without it in the kitchen.

A Cook's Guide to Beer Styles: Flavor First

AMBER ALE – A versatile style for cooking – modest maltiness, hoppiness, caramel notes, and alcohol—with some offering more fruity flavors thanks to the yeasts used in fermentation. Caramel nuances accentuate caramelized flavors developed by grilling with sweet sauces

BARLEY WINE – A very strong ale, almost a liquor, often sweet or thickly malty in taste, yet often strongly bittered. Winter versions may be spiced or flavored with fruits and extracts. Contributes peppery notes from the higher alcohol content. May be reduced into a BBQ sauce with extra sugars such as molasses to offset the hops. Balances strong seasonings such as clove, cinnamon and curry.

BELGIAN & BELGIAN-STYLE GOLDEN ALE – Ranging from strong to very strong, these are very malty, with balanced hops bitterness. American renditions may vary in body, color and hoppiness. The higher alcohol golden or brown ales have sherry notes that make them good for glazes.

BOCK – A dark lager brewed with Bavarian malts, for a deep, bready flavor and malt sweetness. Good to use in sauces with dark brown sugar or honey. Some are high in alcohol with a potency approaching that of barley wine. Excellent with roasted garlic, and its sweetness can augment savory spices such as turmeric, fennel or mustard seed.

BROWN ALE – Big malt flavors balanced with hops bitterness, a brown ale adds more caramel and roasted notes to a recipe. The darker malt content also contributes to faster, darker browning on the grill. Some brown ales have flavors of nuts or fruits so use with complementary flavors such as hazelnut or pecan.

CHIPOTLE OR CHILI ALE – An ale, often an amber or brown ale, infused with chiles during fermentation. If you can't find a bottled version, you may add extra chilies to the recipe to heighten the heat. Use with sauces for beef, vegetables and ribs.

DUBBEL – Abbey ale style, typically brown and malty, with almost syrupy notes. The deep color and raisin sweetness is due to the darkly kilned malts and restrained use of hops in true versions of this style. Good in brines with herbs and caramelized onions.

DUNKEL WEISS – A dark wheat ale made with dark roasted malts to add color and roasty flavor to the weissbier. Often tangy in taste and thicker in body. Adds caramelized colors and flavors; very good with steaks.

ENGLISH MILD ALE – A low-gravity version of an English ale, either amber or brown, reliably less hoppy than American expectations, and balanced in flavor. Excellent with seafood or oysters on the grill.

EXTRA SPECIAL BITTER OR ESB – Generously hopped both in aroma and bitterness, domestics being more aggressive than imports. Higher-alcohol versions intensify sensations of pepper flavors. Use in brines or marinades with zesty herbs such as tarragon or rosemary.

FRUITED ALES –Fruited ales vary greatly, but generally impart big fruit flavors, sweet-tart taste, and character of the fruit used in fermentation, usually with a fairly restrained use of hops. Look for ales brewed with real fruit, not just extracts. Extract flavors can develop off flavors with boiling or heating, so use artificially flavored ales in marinades or glazes. A delicate amber ale mixed with ¼ cup juice concentrate may be used as a substitute for a fruit ale marinades and sauces. Hard ciders are good with fruits and to brine ribs or pork loin. Cherry and raspberry ales are good in marinades or glazes for grilled duck and wild game such as venison. Fruit ales can also serve as an excellent contrast to the flavor notes of hot peppers.

GUEUZE AND LAMBIC – A very tart and complex spontaneously fermented ale, often acidic and aromatic with barnyard-y or lactic notes, and yeasty aromas. Best used in mop sauces to stand in for vinegar. Lambics run the gamut from puckeringly tart to cloyingly sweet, with the tart being truer to tradition. Lambics are made from gueuze with the addition of fruit; see notes under fruit ales. Lambics make delightful vinaigrette-style dressings and mops.

HELLES LAGER – Helles translates as "bright" and these well-balanced straw-colored lagers are somewhat bolder in spicy German hops than mass-market pilsners. Their crispness complements citrus in marinades and mop sauces.

INDIA PALE ALE OR IPA – Citrusy or resinous hops in both aroma and taste, so use caution when heating these beers in a recipe. Often dry-hopped, the hop aromatics accentuate chilies and peppers, and may be used in marinades, glazes and brines.

KÖLSCH ALE – Light, fruity, and delicately hopped, less bitter than the standard pilsner, and a versatile style for bastes and glazes. Also good for steaming sausages.

LAGER – Any bottom-fermented, cold-aged beer, spanning ranges of color, bitterness, maltiness and quality. Most bottled lagers are filtered and pasteurized and lack the aromatics and yeast esters found in many ales. A few recipes call only for "lager," so choose the style you like best.

PALE ALE – A coppery ale, with lots of hops bitterness and often moderately high alcohol. Adds citrus or floral aroma with medium malt body. Good with herbs such as basil or bay leaf.

PILSNER – What many people think of as "beer" often is actually pilsner; however, imported and craft brewed pilsners have much more character, and can be darker and hoppier, especially the Imperial Pilsner styles. Used in lots of sauces, marinades, and glazes.

PORTER – Dark ale, modestly bitter, with espresso to chocolate to toasty flavors. Some Porters, especially domestic microbrews, are flavored with a wide range of additions. Try with molasses, sorghum or maple syrup in barbecue sauces. Good for marinating mushrooms, pork, beef and game.

RAUCHBIER & SMOKED ALES – A German dark lager made with malt smoked over a wood fire, with smoky notes, akin to Lapsang Souchong tea. American interpretations are often porters or stouts, so the dark malt taste can heighten the smoke flavors. A flavorful alternative to liquid smoke, smoked ales add woodsy character to sauces for foods grilled over propane.

RED LAGER – A reddish-copper lager with medium to big malt taste. Sometimes known as Vienna style lager. Mild to moderate hopping, so these can be used in cooked or reduced sauces. Good base for a brine for poultry or fish marinade.

SCOTTISH HEAVY ALE – Malty ale full of raisin, caramel and ripe fruit notes, often very thick body, medium hops bitterness and medium to low carbonation. Excellent as a baste or glaze for grilled mushrooms or beef.

STOUT – Dark ale made with dark roasted barley malts and barley. Variants include silky, dry oatmeal stout, coffee or espresso stouts, fruit stouts such as cherry stout, and sweeter milk stout, with added lactose. All are versatile in sauces and reductions, with ingredients such as roasted garlic, rosemary, and nuts such as walnut or hazelnut.

SUMMER ALE – A quaffable, moderately hopped, quenching style, lower in alcohol than most pale ales, but very crisp. Sometimes spiced with coriander or ginger in homage to the witbier style. Excellent with spices such as cardamom or citrus zests in glazes and bastes. May also be used as a marinade for chicken, especially with mustard and thyme.

TRIPEL – A classic Abbey style, Tripel (like all bottle conditioned beers) undergoes three fermentations (primary, secondary, and in the bottle). Belgian candi sugar provides some of the fermentables, which results in a potent, fruity golden ale. Try a tripel mixed with honey and orange zest in marinades and glazes for vegetables.

WEISS BIER OR WHEAT BEER – Wheat ale, made with malted wheat for a quenching, refreshing character, sometimes with yeast-generated clove, nutmeg, or banana aromatics. American wheat beers tend to be fruitier, with slight astringency, without significant yeast notes. Use with complementary spices such as cinnamon or lemon zest. Good in marinades for chicken and in basting sauces for seafood.

WITBIER – A sub-style of Wheat, popularized in Belgium, brewed with coriander, orange peel, and other exotic spices such as grains of paradise. Big fruity flavors generated in fermentation range from citrusy to slightly tart. Good in brines and marinades. A spritzy contrast when paired with grilled foods, especially seafood.

Index

Adobo Dark Lager Burgers with Roasted Corn Salsa

Grilled Herbed Hazelnut Flatbread

Malty Spice Rub

About the Author

Lucy Saunders writes about beer and food, in newspapers, magazines and books, such as Cooking with Beer (Time Life Books, 1996). She has a degree in Old & Middle English literature, a certificate in web design, studied baking and pastry at the Cooking and Hospitality Institute of Chicago, apprenticed with pub chefs in London and Brussels, and attended the Siebel Institute's seminar on sensory evaluation of beer. She enjoys travel and cooking for friends and family.

Saunders is a certified culinary professional (CCP) member of the International Association of Culinary Professionals. She conducts tastings for groups such as the American Homebrewers Association, the Craft Brewers Conference, the American Cheese Society, and local and regional festivals. She has served as a judge for the Harpoon Championships of New England Barbecue, the American Royal Barbecue Contest in Kansas City, the Austin Chronicle Hot Sauce Competition, and for the Cooking with Beer Challenge sponsored by the National Association of Beer Wholesalers. Her site, beercook.com, won a silver medal for Best Food Writing on the Internet from the Association of Food Journalists in 2002.

Grilling with Beer

Please print legibly

Terms: Payment due with order, allow 3 weeks for processing. With the exception of obvious production defects, no returns.

Name ____________________

Billing Address ____________________

City State Zip ____________________

Country ____________________ Phone ____________________

Email ____________________

Name of Recipient, if different ____________________

If you want book signed, please add the inscription here:

____

Shipping Address ____________________

City State Zip ____________________

Country ____________________ Phone ____________________

Email ____________________

$21.95 per copy, plus applicable sale tax
$5.00 shipping and handling, per book, for U.S. mail delivery. Call for shipping and handling fees for order of more than 3 copies. Extra fees to ship outside United States (FedEx or DHL) or for rush delivery.

_____ **GRILLING WITH BEER $21.95 each** .... $_____
Shipping and handling .... $_____
TOTAL DUE .... $_____

Form of payment:

Certified check or money order, payable to F&B Communications
Credit card *(VISA or Mastercard only, card will be charged when books ship)*

____

Cardholder's name, as it appears on card

Card Number ____________________ Exp. Date ____________

NOTE: All the above information must be completed in order to ship.

FAX order to: Grilling with Beer, 877-790-3930
MAIL order to: Grilling with Beer, Attn: Orders
4230 N. Oakland Ave., #178,
Shorewood, WI 53211

QUESTIONS? Call 1-800-760-5998
or EMAIL grillingwithbeer@yahoo.com

Grilling with Beer

Please print legibly

Terms: Payment due with order, allow 3 weeks for processing. With the exception of obvious production defects, no returns.

Name ______________________________

Billing Address ______________________________

City State Zip ______________________________

Country ______________ Phone______________

Email______________________________

Name of Recipient, if different______________________________

If you want book signed, please add the inscription here:

____

Shipping Address______________________________

City State Zip ______________________________

Country ______________ Phone______________

Email______________________________

$21.95 per copy, plus applicable sale tax
$5.00 shipping and handling, per book, for U.S. mail delivery. Call for shipping and handling fees for order of more than 3 copies. Extra fees to ship outside United States (FedEx or DHL) or for rush delivery.

_____ **GRILLING WITH BEER $21.95 each** .... $_____
Shipping and handling .... $_____
TOTAL DUE .... $_____

Form of payment:

Certified check or money order, payable to F&B Communications
Credit card *(VISA or Mastercard only, card will be charged when books ship)*

____
Cardholder's name, as it appears on card

Card Number______________________________Exp. Date__________

NOTE: All the above information must be completed in order to ship.

FAX order to: Grilling with Beer, 877-790-3930
MAIL order to: Grilling with Beer, Attn: Orders
4230 N. Oakland Ave., #178,
Shorewood, WI 53211

QUESTIONS? Call 1-800-760-5998
or EMAIL grillingwithbeer@yahoo.com